Pretending You Care

Pretending You Care

The Retail Employee Handbook

Norman Feuti

NEW YORK

Library of Congress Cataloging-in-Publication Data has been applied for.

ISBN: 978-1-4013-0890-2

Hyperion books are available for special promotions, premiums, or corporate training. For details contact Michael Rentas, Proprietary Markets, Hyperion, 77 West 66th Street, 12th floor, New York, New York 10023, or call 212-456-0133.

Design by Renato Stanisic

FIRST EDITION

10 9 8 7 6 5 4 3 2 1

To My Wife, Jen, and My Children, Charlotte and Ben

Without Your Patience and Help,
This Book Would Not Be Possible.

Contents

ACKNOWLEDGMENTS XI
INTRODUCTION XIII

CHAPTER **1**
RETAIL MYTHS   1
I'll Get a Good Discount *1*
Working with People Will Be Fun! *3*
Flexible Hours *9*

CHAPTER **2**
HOW TO FIND A TOLERABLE RETAIL JOB   12
Every Retail Job Has Its Own Special Hell *12*
Undercover Work *18*
Hidden Perks *20*

CHAPTER **3**
GETTING HIRED   23
The Application *23*
Your Interviewer Is Faking It *25*
There Are No Right Answers *25*
Personality Tests *28*

CHAPTER **4**

TRAINING 39

Pretending to Read the Handbook *41*
Training Videos: A Laugh Riot! *45*
The Cash Register *58*

CHAPTER **5**

YOUR COWORKERS 67

Being the Newbie *68*
The Archetypes *70*

CHAPTER **6**

THE CUSTOMERS 78

Problem Customers *79*
Unrealistic Expectations *111*
Children: What You Can Be Angry About *122*
Faux Empathy: Pretending You Care *126*
The Customer Is Always Right *127*

CHAPTER **7**

THE PRODUCTS 131

Feigning Product Knowledge *132*
Clearance *134*
Damages *139*

CHAPTER **8**

THE STOCKROOM 143

Pretend Checking *144*
Making Fun of the Customers *147*
Ladders Are for Rookies *151*

CHAPTER **9**

BREAK TIME 155

Location, Location, Location *156*
Exit Strategies *157*
Double Standards: A Short Story *160*
Propaganda *163*

Snack Machines *164*
Turning a Coat Hanger into a Makeshift
Antenna *165*

CHAPTER 10
**ETIQUETTE: HOW NOT TO BE THE
ONE EVERYBODY HATES 167**
Answering the Phone *167*
Paging *169*
Pawning Off Problem Customers and Complaints *170*
Calling in Sick *171*
Recovery *174*

CHAPTER 11
SALES 177
Role-play: It's So Easy When We're Pretending *180*
Taking the Blame *186*
Make It Happen! *187*

CHAPTER 12
MANAGEMENT 190
My Manager Is an Idiot! *191*
Getting Promoted *201*
Conducting Interviews: It's Easier Than You Think *206*
Sales Meetings *208*
The District Manager Visit *210*
Action Plans: Punishment in the Form
of Creative Writing *212*

CHAPTER 13
THE CORPORATE OFFICE 215
People Who Have Never Worked at the Store Level *217*
Micromanagement: We Don't Know Who
Our Employees Are! *221*
"Incentives" *227*
~~Spies~~ Secret Shoppers *232*
The VP Visit *235*

CHAPTER 14

LOSS PREVENTION 241
Shrink *242*
Shoplifting *245*
Turning in Your Friends for Fun and Profit *249*
Inventory: Please God, Kill Me *250*

CHAPTER 15

THE MALL 256
The Hierarchy of Stores *256*
Security *258*
Parking *261*

CHAPTER 16

CHRISTMAS 266
"Happy Holidays" *267*
The 120 Days of Christmas *268*
Christmas Help *270*
Toys Worth Trampling For *276*
Crushed Christmas Spirits *280*

CHAPTER 17

G.O.B. (GOING OUT OF BUSINESS) 283
Why This Is the Best Thing That Could Happen to You *283*
Just Deserts: A Short Story *290*
Free Stuff! *294*

EPILOGUE 295

Acknowledgments

I would like to thank Glenn Mott, the director of publishing at King Features, and Zareen Jaffery, my editor at Hyperion, for their hard work in helping me to make this book a reality.

I would also like to give a special thanks to the late Jay Kennedy. Jay was the editor-in-chief of King Features Syndicate and was the man who gave me my shot at being a syndicated cartoonist.

Cartooning is an esoteric industry, so when you're submitting ideas for syndication it's difficult to know whether you're on the right track or not. When everyone else sent me form rejection letters, Jay Kennedy took time out of his incredibly busy day to call me on the phone and give me advice on how to make my strip better. The result of his generosity was a more focused submission that eventually became the *Retail* comic strip that is the impetus for this book.

When someone as big as Jay Kennedy takes the time to give an absolute nobody like me pointers over the phone, it leaves an impression. I owe him a debt of gratitude for rescuing me from the retail trenches and launching my own dream career.

Jay was monumentally respected in the industry and I'm honored to have had the opportunity to work with him. He will be sorely missed.

Introduction

WHY DO YOU THINK WE TAKE SO MUCH ABUSE FROM PEOPLE, MARLA?

WELL, WE LIVE IN A SOCIETY THAT COVETS MATERIAL POSSESSIONS.

SO, AS RETAIL EMPLOYEES, OUR ACTIONS CAN HAVE A PROFOUND EFFECT ON A PERSON'S SENSE OF WELL-BEING. SUBCONSCIOUSLY, THEY RESENT THE POWER WE HAVE OVER THEIR HAPPINESS.

WOW, THAT'S DEEP.

YEAH, WELL, THAT AND MOST PEOPLE ARE JERKS.

I am of the opinion that everyone should hold a retail job at least once in their life—not because I think it's an enjoyable experience, but because I think it builds empathy for the human condition. I believe that working in retail for more than fifteen years has taught me a lot about people and the world we live in. The things I've learned are not always pretty, but they are valuable and true nonetheless.

Throughout this book of handy advice and cartoons, I have inserted many personal experiences from my own illustrious retail career. While many of the names have been changed to protect the guilty, I assure you the stories themselves are true.

I hope this book will comfort those who work in retail, and enlighten those who do not. If this book helps to make just one retail worker's next open-to-close shift a little easier, then it's all worth it.

Enjoy.

Pretending You Care

CHAPTER 1

Retail Myths

Before we begin, I feel it's appropriate to dispel the three most common myths about working in retail. Many retail organizations are all too happy to tout these pseudo-benefits as bona fide incentives for obtaining a retail job, but don't be fooled!

If you decide to get a retail job, don't do it for a bunch of empty promises. Do it on your own terms.

I'LL GET A GOOD DISCOUNT

One of the biggest misconceptions about retail employees is that they receive a generous discount on merchandise. Nothing could be farther from the truth. Consider the following:

Typically, a retail employee receives somewhere between a

20 and 30 percent discount on merchandise, but there are usu-
ally a few caveats tacked on to significantly limit the way it can
be used. The discount can't be used on top of a sale, or on
clearance items, or on select merchandise that would amount
to what the store considers exorbitant or "unfair" savings,
etc. . . .

If you still think that's pretty decent, contrast it with the average coupon a store offers to the general public on a regular
basis:

Typically, a coupon gives the customer somewhere between
a 20 and 30 percent discount on merchandise, but there are
usually a few caveats tacked on to significantly limit the way it
can be used. A coupon can't be used on top of a sale, or on
clearance items, or on select merchandise that would amount
to what the store considers exorbitant or "unfair" savings,
etc. . . .

Basically, what most retailers call an employee discount
amounts to nothing more than a perpetual coupon. Every
major retailer runs a sale and/or distributes a coupon at least
every other week, so at best your employee discount will only
give you the minor benefit of not having to wait a week to get
the same discount anyone off the street can get.

This might not be a deal breaker for you. But, if it's your only
incentive for seeking out a retail job, you may want to reconsider. If, on the other hand, being spared the hassle of ever having to cut coupons out of the newspaper for the one particular
store you want to work at appeals to you, then you're in luck.

To be fair, there is the rare retail job that does offer a larger
discount to employees. But the ones that do are generally in the
business of ripping off the customer big time, so the larger discount is relative.

Jewelry stores are a good example. A store employee might
be able to buy a $199 pendant for $50, but that same pendant
will be perpetually on sale for $99. Not to mention that the
thing only costs like $10. So, unless the idea of being ripped
off *less* appeals to you, this is no great prize either.

WORKING WITH PEOPLE WILL BE FUN!

If you're a friendly person and have never had to deal with the general public in any official capacity before, you may have the notion that working with people will be enjoyable. When you think of "people," you probably think of your family, friends, and neighbors—the nice folks you've surrounded yourself with throughout life. In your own small, insular corner of the world, greetings are reciprocated, help is appreciated, and good will is universal, so you may find it natural to expect the rest of the world to conform to these expectations.

Let me tell you, my friend, that you are sadly mistaken.

If you think working with the general public will be fun, you're obviously naïve, but I won't pick on you. You're a nice person who just hasn't taken your lumps in life yet. It's nothing to be ashamed of. But I do feel it's my duty to make sure you have realistic expectations before you head off into the retail jungle armed with nothing more than a smile and a good attitude.

Recommended Viewing

If you want to gain a little perspective on what it's going to be like working with the general public, sit down and watch some daytime reality television for a few days in a row. *Jerry Springer*, *Dr. Phil*, *Maury*, *Judge Joe Brown*—watch all of that stuff. While you're at it, be sure to end each night by watching your local 11 o'clock news as well. Then, after you're done recoiling in disgust at the new low humanity has sunk to, take a moment to reflect on something. All of those people shop.

That's right. Let it sink in.

The guy on the news whose house was filled with garbage and animal carcasses, the crazy mom who makes her six-year-old daughter compete in those freaky child beauty pageants, the toothless meth-head who's sleeping with his girlfriend's mother, the guy being sued by his ex-fiancée for a $1,600 cell phone bill and bail money—they *all* shop.

"Child-pageant mom" needs to buy lots of makeup. "Garbage-house guy" needs to buy random trinkets to chuck on the kitchen floor. "Meth-head" needs to shoplift to support his habit. They *all* head out to the mall at some point, and guess what? It's only a matter of time before you're going to have to wait on one of them.

You think about that.

Testimonials

If you're still unconvinced that working with people is in fact *not* fun, then you'll probably just have to find out for yourself. But, in a last ditch effort to educate you, I'll share a couple of real-life experiences I've had in an attempt to drive the point home.

You may think problems only happen when there is a conflict—not true. When you're working with the public, you're not only going to have to deal with real problems, you're also going to have to deal with imaginary ones. The world is filled with people who have issues that you will never see coming.

The Invisible Chip on My Shoulder

Back in the late '90s I worked as the store manager of a small men's shoe store in a mall. I was working alone one afternoon and, as was customary during the slower day shift, I was keeping busy by dusting the tables and polishing the display shoes.

During my chores, two gentlemen entered together, and as they did, I greeted them with a cordial "Hi, how are you?" The men made eye contact with me, but did not return my greeting. They then proceeded to a rack of shoes and began to discuss them in low tones. Since this kind of slight is commonplace, I thought nothing of it and continued with my cleaning.

I worked on commission, so I was of course keen to make any sale. But experience has told me that the type of customer who ignores your greeting is turned off by anything resembling high-pressure selling, so it's best to let them look, and come to you when they're ready. So I made sure not to hover over the two men looking at shoes, but I remained aware of them and ready to help when and if they needed it. Keep in mind that the store was very small. It was a corner store with a thin sales floor measuring about 300 square feet. So, as I puttered about doing my chores, there was never a point when I was more than fifteen feet from the two men.

Before I continue, it's important to note one fact about shoe stores. When a customer is shopping in a full-service shoe store and is ready to try on a shoe, they will pick up said shoe, hold it aloft, and look at the nearest salesperson. Usually, they'll also say something to the salesperson like, "Can I get this in a size 9?" or, "I'd like to try this on." Sometimes they just look at the salesperson and say nothing, but they always hold up the shoe. It's the universal way to indicate that you want to try one on. You can walk into any shoe store in the world and prompt service by picking up a shoe, holding it at about shoulder level, and making eye contact with the nearest salesperson.

This never happened. At no point did either of the two men hold up a shoe, or make eye contact with me, or ask me a question. They just looked at the shoes and discussed them among themselves.

After about three or four minutes, the two men left. Not an uncommon event at all. Throughout any given day, many people would enter the store, look at some shoes, and then leave without trying anything on or asking any questions. I happened to be cleaning a table near the entrance as they were leaving, so I said, "Have a nice day." The two men got about ten feet out into the mall before one of them turned to me and said, "Maybe I'll come back and buy the whole store."

Thinking this was some lame attempt at humor, I offered the man the fake yet convincing smile I've perfected over the years to indicate to him that I got and appreciated the joke—even though I didn't. Apparently it wasn't meant as a joke however, because the man stopped dead in his tracks and angrily said, "Oh, you don't believe me?"

That caught me off guard, so all I could manage to come up with was a blank stare and a confused "Uh."

At that point he marched up to me and stuck his finger accusingly in my face. "What, you think I don't have any money? Huh? You take one look at me and assume I can't afford your shoes! Maybe I have enough money to buy this whole store!" The man he was with said nothing, but stood close by with his arms crossed and a look on his face that suggested he was in agreement with his friend.

Stunned, I said, "What are you talking about?"

"How do you know I'm not a millionaire?" was his reply. "For all you know, I could come back and buy ten pairs of shoes!"

In spite of the fact that this man's tirade against me was unjustified, out of left field, and completely a product of his own insecurity, I couldn't help but think what a ridiculous notion that was. Our average pair of shoes cost about $80. Certainly more than some would care to spend on such things, but hardly the stuff of champagne dreams and caviar wishes. You didn't need to be anywhere near a millionaire to shop at our store.

"Um, *okay*," I said, baffled.

"You don't deserve my business!" said the man. Then, with a final look of disgust he grabbed his sympathetic buddy and stormed off, leaving me in a funk for the rest of the day.

Not fun.

Creep

This incident took place during the time I was working for the same shoe store chain, but this time I was helping out in a new store they had opened in a different mall. The wife of the manager of this new store had just had a baby, so all the store managers in the district, including myself, were chipping in by pulling a couple of shifts in his store so he could take a week off.

On the day in question, I opened the store and another manager came in to close. It was a slow day, so no other help was needed. During the overlap in our shifts, I went to the food court to get lunch.

I went to this Chinese place, the name of which I have forgotten. After a brief wait in line, I ordered some General Tso's chicken with a side of vegetables and pork fried rice. Good stuff.

I hate eating in the food court, so I took my food back to the store to eat in the back room. When I returned to the store, my coworker was helping a customer. I got about three steps inside when someone yelled, *"Hey!"* from the mall corridor.

Naturally, I turned around to see who had yelled, as did my coworker and his customer. Standing in front of the store was a short, bespectacled old woman whom I had never seen before. She had a contemptuous scowl on her face and was looking directly and unmistakably at me.

"What the hell's wrong with you?" she yelled. "Passing me like that! What are you, some kind of creep?"

Stunned, I looked around. "Are you talking to me?" I asked incredulously.

"You think you're a real hot shot don't you?" she continued. "You creep!"

Not sure what to say and painfully aware that passersby in the mall, my coworker, and his customer were all watching this exchange and wondering what I did to this poor old woman, I just stood agape with my Chinese food.

My mind frantically tried to figure out what she could be talking about. *"Passing me like that"*? I've never seen this lady before! Had I passed her in the mall? If I had, it's not like I sprinted back from the food court and some near collision happened between us that I thoughtlessly ignored. I walked at a normal pace and didn't so much as brush up against anyone. The trip was completely uneventful. I'm sure I would remember if I had stiff-armed an elderly woman within the last ten minutes. What was this lady talking about? Was she mad because I was simply walking faster than her? Was she angry that I dared to flaunt my unbridled youth by breezing past her in a thirty-foot-wide hallway? Did she imagine me snickering to myself as I left her in my dust? Did she expect that anyone walking behind her in the mall should have slowed down to seventy-year-old woman speed? I couldn't even fathom.

After another moment of hateful staring and one more "You creep!" the old woman finally wandered away mumbling angrily and leaving me to hopelessly contemplate the nature of her psychosis.

My coworker looked at me with concern and a raised eyebrow. "Geez Norm, what the hell did you do to her?"

Flustered, I said, "I have no idea! I've never seen her before in my life!"

My coworker and his customer exchanged a brief glance before going back to their business.

I don't think either of them believed me.

Not fun.

FLEXIBLE HOURS

First, lets take a look at the word "flexible."

flexible | ˈflek.sə.bəl |
adjective
able to be easily modified to respond to altered
circumstances or conditions

To believe that a retail job will offer you "flexible" hours is to believe that any employer would allow you to dictate your own schedule. Either they can accommodate your schedule or they can't, but no employer is going to modify his or her own needs to meet yours. That's just not realistic.

The truth of the matter is that retail jobs don't offer any more flexibility than any other job—they just have a wider range of hours available because they are open nights and weekends. It's ideal employment if you can't work a regular job because you're attending school, or have children, or whatnot. But, whatever your availability is, your employer is going to hold you to it. If you say you're available Friday nights, you can expect to be working on Friday nights whenever they need you to—which in retail is always.

On the other hand, your retail employer is going to expect *you* to be plenty flexible. You're going to have to work on weekends and holidays. Your schedule is going to change from week to week. The number of hours you work in a given week is going to fluctuate based on sales. If something comes up and you can't work a day that you're scheduled to work, then that's just tough. Find someone to cover your shift, or make other arrangements. There are no sick days in retail.

I don't know anyone working in retail who wouldn't rather work 9 to 5, Monday through Friday, and have weekends off. Don't get me wrong—it's not an entirely bad deal. It's nice to have a weekday off and be able to sleep in often, but to imply that it's some kind of perk is just ridiculous.

"You mean I get to work on Friday and Saturday night while everyone else I know goes out? Sweet! What a bonus!"

Ever notice that no one ever writes songs about how cool it is to party on Wednesday nights? They don't because it's not.

Quick Tips

We'll discuss the best way to obtain a retail job later, but since we're on the subject, here are a couple of easy tricks to gaining a little bit of real flexibility in a new retail job.

Tip 1

When you fill out an application for a retail job, there will be a section that asks you which days you can work. Indicate that you can't work at all on Mondays.

Since Monday is the slowest shopping day of the week, a retail employer won't care that you can't work it, so it won't affect your chances of getting the job. But more important, you will get out of having to work any of the Monday holidays on a technicality.

Labor Day, Memorial Day, Veterans' Day . . . stores don't close on any of those holidays anymore. Add the fact that most states don't require companies to pay anything extra to the retail employees who do work on those holidays, and there's no reason you would want to miss your family barbeque to wait on people who choose to waste the day shopping.

Initially, your employer may ask you to supply a reason why you can't work on Mondays. Just make sure whatever you make up is something that no one would feel comfortable asking you to get out of—like volunteering at a nursing home, or teaching orphans how to read.

Tip 2

The second tip is really just supplemental to the first. Pick one more day that you can't work when you apply. It can be any day other than Friday, Saturday, or Sunday.

This is your five-day-or-less workweek guarantee. Because if you don't have that second day that you absolutely can't work because of those poor illiterate orphans you tutor, you're leaving yourself open to working the occasional six days in a row when your employer is short-handed.

I recommend you choose Thursday, because it also guarantees you will never have to work more than three days in a row without a day off.

CHAPTER 2

How to Find a Tolerable Retail Job

I f you're looking for your first retail job, this chapter will help you hedge your bets and find a place to work that will cause you as little grief as possible. If you already have a retail job that is causing you a lot of grief, then this chapter will help you find a better one. If you've already worked in retail way too long and are hanging up the towel for the corporate sector, then I can't help you. Go read *On the Fast Track*, or *Dilbert*, or something.

EVERY RETAIL JOB HAS ITS OWN SPECIAL HELL

Before you begin your search for the perfect retail job, there is one important fact that you need to understand—there isn't one.

This chapter isn't going to help you locate retail nirvana because it doesn't exist. The goal here is to help you find a *tolerable* retail job, not one that is completely hassle free—that's just a pipe dream. There are crappy retail jobs and there are *really* crappy retail jobs, but there are no retail jobs that are crap-free. It's a fact, and the sooner you accept it, the better off you'll be.

Trust me, I've worked for a plethora of different retail establishments and each one of them had its own special way of making you regularly interact with the customers in an unpleasant way.

Your Own Personal Inferno

Hell is different for everybody. What is torture for some is merely uncomfortable for others. In an effort to help you make an informed decision about where to apply for a job, I've supplied a short list of the more common unpleasant retail duties and the types of stores usually associated with them.

You have to expect some degree of misery in any retail environment, but hopefully this list will help you avoid some of the more objectionable retail responsibilities that you may not have thought of.

Carding for Cigarettes
Convenience Stores, Gas Stations, Grocery Stores

Anytime you have to question the honesty of a customer, it's going to create an uncomfortable situation and potential conflict. Especially when said customer is in fact *not* being honest. So when you work in a store that sells cigarettes, you can expect this potential conflict to occur over and over again throughout the course of any given day.

Having to ask for proof of age when selling cigarettes creates three distinct hassles for a cashier. First, many of the customers who look younger than they are will take offense at being asked to show their I.D. and will be sure to let you know just how off the mark they think your perception is. They won't care that you're just doing your job, or that getting caught selling cigarettes to a minor would cost you a $500 fine and possibly get you fired. They'll only care that their precious ego was bruised and they'll be sure to make an attempt at bruising yours in retaliation.

"I.D.? I'm 22! Did you forget your glasses or are you just retarded?"

The second hassle happens when you have to deny cigarettes to customers who fail to produce I.D. No matter how you feel about smoking in general, be assured that denying an individual the addictive substance they crave is never going to end amicably. Prepare to be cursed at, flipped off, or worse.

Add the third hassle of having to endure the neverending litany of lame excuses that minors will use in an attempt to convince you to turn a blind eye, and you have a trifecta of suck.

My favorite excuse is "I left my license in the car." Aside from the fact that it's a ridiculously easy bluff to call someone on, you'd have to have absolutely no practical experience in the world to believe it. Have you ever met anyone who didn't carry their I.D. in their wallet? Seriously, who just chucks their license and credit cards on the dashboard or passenger seat? The entire premise is patently absurd.

Selling Extended Warranties
Computer/Electronics Sales, Jewelry Stores

Working for a store that offers extended warranties or service plans on its products can be a headache. Selling a warranty is much different from selling a physical thing. Warranties and service plans are intangibles and Joe Average tends to have the preconceived notion that such things are a rip-off.

You can argue the legitimacy of service plans all you want, but most people view them as a con and you're going to have to deal with that attitude when you sell them. No matter how much you believe in them, the vast majority of customers are going to give you a smug look that says, *"Save it, Slick, you can't sucker me,"* then cut you off in mid sentence with a firm, *"No!"*

Since extended warranties amount to a lot of free money for retailers, another part of the hassle is that you will constantly be under the gun to sell them. In most cases your job will literally depend on meeting a company standard or quota. So it's a drudgery you can't avoid.

The only saving grace of selling extended warranties is that occasionally one of those smug jerks who blew off your pitch will come back a few months later with his tail between his legs and a busted laptop. Then you get to tell him that he's SOL.

Sweet as it is when it happens, it's a rare occurrence. You have to decide for yourself whether the mere possibility of witnessing such poetic justice is worth the daily aggravation.

Pushing "Rewards Cards"
Book Stores, Office Supply Stores, Supermarkets, Drugstores
Many retailers now offer some kind of "rewards" card to their patrons. While these cards are touted as a way for their most valued shoppers to receive special deals and savings, they are really just a way to trick consumers into giving up personal information in exchange for the same old sales and coupons the store used to give out to everyone.

Strangely, these cards are far better received than the moribund mailing lists of the past. Consumers don't seem to mind that the local grocery store is earmarking them as a potential terrorist whenever they buy a lot of curry or couscous, just so long as they aren't sending them a bunch of junk mail.

But it isn't the potentially dark nature of the rewards card that will be a hassle, it's the additional time it takes to complete a transaction. At the end of every sale, you either have to sign up a new member or wait painfully while an existing member fumbles through their purse or wallet to find your store's card among a stack of others'.

Meanwhile, the retailer isn't going to supply any extra pay-roll hours to deal with the added procedure and they definitely won't allow you to skip the step, even when it's busy. So when a line does form at the register, it just keeps getting longer and an-grier. Then, when you have to continue asking all the people who've been stewing in line if they want to join the "Super Happy Fun Club," they blow up at you.

The horror of it all is that you'll see those angry faces com-ing and you'll know there's going to be an explosion, but you'll have to ask anyway.

Cleaning Public Restrooms
Various
No matter what its system is, if you choose to work at a store with public restrooms, you're eventually going to draw the short straw and get stuck cleaning them. Even the retail chains that hire illegal immigrants to clean the restrooms don't keep them on staff 24/7. If an "accident" happens midday or early in the morning, some unlucky employee is going to have to clean up human waste—and that someone could be you.

If you work in a bookstore with public restrooms, you'll have the added bonus of retrieving discarded pornography from the stalls on a nightly basis. It's amazing how adept you can become at getting a wrinkled copy of *Penthouse* off a wet bathroom floor and into the trash using nothing but a mop handle.

Sorry, did I say "amazing"? I meant "nightmarish."

Touching People's Feet
Full-Service Shoe Stores, Haberdasheries
Although the experienced salesman can shoe a customer without making physical contact with the foot, it takes practice to perfect the technique. If you take a job at a full-service shoe store or haberdashery, be prepared to come into contact with the feet of the masses while you learn the ropes.

If you have dry skin or eczema you might seriously consider avoiding this type of work altogether, because you're going to repeat a routine of washing your hands then dunking them in a bucket of Purell about every twenty minutes.

I know nobody uses the word "haberdashery" anymore, but they should.

UNDERCOVER WORK

So you've read the shortlist and you think you've found a store that you can live with. Not so fast. Simply knowing whether a store has a rewards card or a public restroom is nowhere near enough research. You need to do some undercover work before you make the decision to fill out an application.

You can learn a lot about a store by shopping there—or at least pretending to shop there. You should visit a store at least two times incognito before making your decision.

Things to Look Out For

Here are some things to look out for when you're doing your undercover work.

Making Fun of the Manager

If you're lucky enough to overhear some employees complaining about what a jerk the manager is, be sure to listen in. If you think their complaints are legitimate, you've just saved yourself the headache of working for a jerk. If you suspect their complaints are baseless, then you have potential blackmail material when you get the job and need to pick up some extra hours.

It's a win/win situation.

Snooty Merchandise = Snooty Customers

How upscale are the products the store sells? Imagine what your annual income would need to be to comfortably afford them. $100,000? $200,000? $300,000?

It's a proven scientific fact that the more money you have, the farther removed you are from reality and the more unrealistic your expectations are. If the store caters to rich people, you can expect an exponential increase in the amount of bogus customer service issues that are going to crop up.

I'll share some real doozies later on.

Bombshell Employees

This is counterintuitive, but if there are too many really attractive employees working in the store, then don't apply there. A store that is filled with supermodel wannabes is going to attract supermodel wannabe customers and repel normal people.

Watch a single episode of *The Simple Life*, then ask yourself if you want to work with and wait on a bunch of mean-spirited Paris Hilton clones all day. You know what stores I'm talking about.

Stop kidding yourself. They wouldn't hire you anyway.

Shoplifters' Paradise

Is the security in the store so lax that you could simply walk out with anything and the employees wouldn't notice? Is the store so sparsely staffed that it would be impossible for the employees to curtail shoplifting by any reasonable margin?

If the answer to these questions is yes, then you should keep moving. You don't want their problem to be your problem. Unless you're a thief, in which case you would gladly become part *of* the problem.

Of course if you *are* a thief, then you probably stole this book. So, I have nothing more to say to you . . . dirtbag!

Proximity to the Food Court

If the store you're looking at is in a mall, then its proximity to the food court should be considered.

Ideally, you want to work in a store that is neither too close nor too far away from the food court. If the store is too far away, you're going to waste valuable break time walking to and from the food court. If the store is too close, you're going to end up sharing any insect or rodent problems they might have.

Let's face it, the food court is only enjoyable as long as you remain blissfully ignorant of the huge freakin' cockroaches that live there.

Children's Videos
If the store sells children's videos and DVDs they probably run a sample video or "mix tape" of their selection somewhere in the store for atmosphere. A variety of small monitors randomly spread about the store is okay, but if there is one central, giant monitor that plays a continual loop of children's songs or some kid's television program, it will slowly drive you insane.

You can only hear "Hakuna Matata" so many times before you snap and start pelting children with stuffed animals.

I could name all the Teletubbies and sing the theme to *Blue's Clues* long before I had kids—and that's just wrong.

HIDDEN PERKS
Let's take a break from the doom and gloom for a minute and look for the silver lining in the dark cloud of retail. Even though your employer isn't going to offer any real benefits, there are some hidden perks out there if you know where to look.

Keep an eye out for these advantages during your search.

A Manager Who Smokes
A store with a manager who smokes can present an advantage for anyone if you know how to play it. Of course, if *you* smoke, the manager will be sympathetic to your needs and let you take frequent smoke breaks. But even if you don't smoke, you can use all the extra ten-minute breaks your manager sneaks in throughout the day as an excuse to justify your own behavior.

Whenever he or she gives you a hard time about tardiness, long lunches, or leaving early, all you have to do is get all indignant and say, *"Oh, I suppose if I smoked cigarettes I could come and go as I please!"* After that the subject will usually be dropped.

Collectible Toys

A store that sells toys may present you with the opportunity to capitalize on the next collectible that comes along. Every few years another Beanie Babies or Pokemon craze pops up—and when it does, you'll find yourself in a position of power.

On shipment day, you and your coworkers will gain virtual VIP status. Mall employees and customers alike will clamber to gain your favor in the hopes that you will grace them with your inside knowledge. You might even be offered free stuff in exchange for putting one of those special toys aside.

I used to hold those special "bear" Beanie Babies for the manager of the Chinese place in the food court of the mall where I once worked. In exchange, he gave me free food whenever I wanted! Tell me that's not awesome. All I had to do was put them aside for him. He didn't even want me to steal them—and I might have seriously considered it for free Chinese food.

You also have the potential to make extra cash by hoarding those toys for yourself. Buy the "good ones" with your meager discount, then sell them for a killing on eBay.

Shopping Carts

For some reason, a lot of people don't like rounding up the carriages. Those people are missing a golden opportunity to slack in a very undetectable fashion.

Want some fresh air or a smoke? Do a cart run.

Want to do some quick shopping? Do a cart run.

Want to listen to the radio in your car? Do a cart run.

Want to avoid some real work? Do a cart run.

The beauty of the cart run is that there is always a stray cart or two that has rolled all the way to the far corner of the parking lot, so you always have a ready and believable excuse to explain what took you so long. Just keep one beat-up carriage hidden behind a lamppost or Dumpster and wheel it out when you're ready to go back to work.

"Sorry I was gone so long. I saw one of our carts out on the interstate, so I figured I should go get it."

Large Sales Floor

A store with a large labyrinth of a sales floor will provide you with daily opportunities to avoid work. Unless someone is actively searching for you, you can kill up to an hour doing nothing but laps around the store. But remember to keep moving! As long as you are in motion, it won't look as if you're slacking. If the boss should unexpectedly turn the corner and find you reading a magazine or eating an apple, you're screwed.

You can also use a large sales floor to hide from your supervisor when you know he or she has an unpleasant job for you. Although an experienced manager isn't going to waste too much time playing hide and seek, once you're paged over the intercom, the game is over.

The best use of a big sales floor is ditching problem customers. As soon as the time comes to direct them to a product, just bob and weave through the aisles at full speed until you've lost them.

We'll talk about problem customers later. Trust me.

CHAPTER 3

Getting Hired

Once you've found the most tolerable retail job you can, the next step is to actually get hired. This chapter contains invaluable advice on how to present yourself in the most desirable light to a prospective retail employer.

THE APPLICATION

Obviously, the first thing you need to do to get a retail job is to fill out an application. While this process is fairly straightforward, it is important to know how the average store manager will evaluate the information you provide.

Here are a few tips to follow when filling out an application that will increase your chances of landing an interview.

Availability

No matter what your availability is during the week, you must be available to work Friday nights and all day on Saturdays and Sundays. Okay, you don't really have to be available those days, but you need to say you are to get an interview. A manager will throw Mr. Too-good-to-work-on-Saturday's application right in the trash.

May We Contact Your Former Employer?

Always check "yes" no matter what your former boss thinks of you.

Don't worry about getting a bad reference from the last place you worked. Checking references is a crappy job, so retail managers always pawn it off on their assistants . . . who in turn will only pretend to check them because they're too busy. So odds are that no one will ever call your former employer. Even on the off chance that they do, most retailers make it a policy not to say anything about previous employees except the dates they were employed—so you're covered.

If you check the box that says "no," the manager is just going to assume that you did something shady at your last job and move on. Call their bluff on this one.

Salary Desired

Nothing other than "negotiable" should be written in this space. Writing any monetary amount is just unnecessarily hurting your chances of getting hired. The manager will assume that you aren't willing to work for less than whatever figure you supply, so why write anything? I guarantee you that they pay less than what you would desire, so don't waste your time.

Spelling

Nothing makes a retail manager feel better than a college student who misspells the word "college." He'll get this smug and superior look on his face, then parade that application around to any employee who cares to look. Later, he'll chuck that application right in the old circular file, secure in the knowledge that higher education is a waste of money.

Education
College has two Ls. Otherwise, it's not particularly relevant.

YOUR INTERVIEWER IS FAKING IT
Hopefully, once you have filled out your application in the best possible way, you will be called back to the store for an interview.

Your interview will take place either on a mall bench or in the store manager's "office," where the occasional employee will pass through and throw you a look that says, "Oh, you poor bastard, you have no idea what you're getting yourself into." In the latter case, don't let it throw you. Focus on the goal at hand. First you need to get the job. You can learn how to deal with its depressing nature later.

Your interviewer is going to ask you a bunch of open-ended questions that were culled from an HR manual. The way you answer these questions is supposed to reveal a lot about your character, but the truth is the manager doesn't really know or care what these questions are supposed to reveal about you. He or she is only interested in seeing if you can answer the questions at all and if you will say something monumentally stupid while doing so.

In short, your interviewer is faking it. A retail manager doesn't have time for a lot of psychological mumbo-jumbo. All that's really important is that you are able to make up a plausible answer to a difficult question on the spot without putting your foot in your mouth.

That's what customer service is all about.

THERE ARE NO RIGHT ANSWERS
Even though your storytelling ability is being judged in the interview more than your character, it's important to be cautious. Re-

member, your interviewer is also listening to see if you say something stupid.

There are no right answers to the questions you will be asked, but there are definitely *wrong* ones. If you answer even one of these questions in the absolute wrong way, you won't get the job. So you need to be aware of what those wrong answers are.

Otherwise what you say isn't too important.

Here are a few common questions you are likely to be asked, and how you *shouldn't* respond to them.

Where do you see yourself in five years?

Where you see yourself down the road doesn't really matter. Whether you say you want to be an astronaut or join the circus, your interviewer doesn't care. You just have to say something. If you're at least working toward some kind of pipe dream, you'll be perceived as less likely to bolt in a week when you find out the job sucks.

The only wrong answer to this question is:

"I don't know."

Look, if you don't have a dream, you're going to have to make one up. Telling your interviewer you have no idea where you might be in five years is like telling them you're a drifter. You might as well wear a dirty trenchcoat and bring along a bottle of gin in a paper bag.

Where you pretend to see yourself in five years isn't important, so long as you pretend to see yourself somewhere. If you want to get anywhere in life, you've got to pretend to have goals.

What's your greatest strength?

A lot of people tend to blurt out the wrong answer to this question right away.

"I'm good with customers!"

Man, that's a stupid thing to say. That statement tells your interviewer that you delude yourself into thinking you have some degree of control over the customer. Unless you can do the Jedi mind trick, you're not "good with customers." You're just cordial enough not to piss people off under normal circumstances—and that's not a strength, it's a prerequisite of the job.

We'll talk more about the customers in Chapter 6. For now, just remove the phrase *"good with customers"* from your vocabulary.

What's your greatest weakness?

There are plenty of *bad* answers to this question. Such as:

"I have a short fuse."

"I have a weak bladder."

"Weed."

But I'll assume that you're smart enough to avoid divulging your real weakness. Barring that, the only dead *wrong* answer is:

"I have no weaknesses."

If you think your interviewer is going to be impressed with your bold confidence, you are sadly mistaken. Your interviewer is only going to be impressed with what an arrogant dork you are.

Personally, I always answer "Kryptonite." It hasn't failed me yet.

Tell me about a time when you had to work with someone who was difficult to get along with.

Again, there are plenty of bad answers to this question, but I'm going to assume you won't tell them about the time you keyed a coworker's car after he stole your commission on a sale.

The wrong answer here is:

"I talked to my manager about it and he helped resolve the issue."

That just makes you sound like a whiner. The store manager is a busy person. The last thing he or she wants to deal with is your bellyaching every time a coworker looks at you funny.

Deal with your own problems, you baby.

Tell me about a time when you delivered great customer service.

There isn't so much a wrong answer to this question as there is a wrong way to end it. You can either make up a scenario out of whole cloth, or you can simply embellish upon one of the few moments from your last job when you were actually allowed to focus solely on the customers. But whatever you do, don't end your story with:

". . . and the customer was very appreciative."

The customer who openly appreciates your best efforts is as rare as the spotted owl. Your interviewer already suspects you are lying on this question. Adding an appreciative customer to the end of your fairy tale will just put it over the top and kill your credibility.

Even if you tell a real story and the customer actually was appreciative, pretend that he wasn't.

PERSONALITY TESTS

More and more retail chains are using personality testing to screen prospective employees. In the corporate world personality tests are used to judge everything from communication skills to career aptitude. In the retail world they are basically used to judge one thing—how likely you are to steal.

The retail version of the personality test generally consists of about one hundred multiple-choice questions. The way you answer those questions yields a percentage. The higher the percentage, the more "honest" you are. The lower your percentage, the more "dishonest" you are.

Of course, the biggest downfall of these tests is that they assume you are answering the questions honestly. If you ask me, any test that asks you to tell the truth about how dishonest you are is inherently flawed.

Why You Should Lie About Your Honesty

The most important thing you need to realize when taking a personality test is that the more questions you answer honestly, the lower your score will be. That's not to say that you can't pass the test by answering all the questions honestly, but you are definitely hurting your odds. Here is a question from an actual test I once took for a job that illustrates the point perfectly.

> Have you ever known anyone who ever took anything
> that didn't belong to them?
> ( ) *Yes*
> ( ) *No*

The mistake most people make when they take a personality test is to overthink a question like this and try to figure out what the answer is supposed to determine about them.

"Hmmm," they think to themselves. "Have I *ever* known *anyone* who *ever* took *anything* that didn't belong to them? Of course I have. Who could honestly answer that question with a no? I wouldn't believe anyone who said they hadn't. This question must be designed to gauge whether I'll answer honestly, or just tell them what I think they want to hear. They're trying to trick me into lying. I'll choose yes."

While that reasoning makes sense in the real world, you have to realize that this test was created by people who don't live in the real world (*See Chapter 13: The Corporate Office*). Every question on the personality test has a hidden subtext. What they're really asking you is:

> *Do you hang out with thieves?*
> ( ) *Yes*
> ( ) *No*

Of course no one would be dumb enough to answer that question with a yes. So the question has been rephrased in a harmless yet equally unambiguous way in order to elicit a genuine response. In doing this, the question loses its original spirit and becomes essentially meaningless, but the test isn't about making sense—it's about making the people in the home office think they have a magic formula to weed out undesirables.

Another thing you should be aware of is that the test operates on the theory that your view of the world reflects upon your own behavior. So when the test asks you:

> *What percentage of people do you think would steal if they thought they wouldn't be caught?*
> ( ) *0–10%*
> ( ) *10–30%*
> ( ) *30–60%*
> ( ) *60–80%*
> ( ) *90–100%*

What they're really asking you is:

> *As a percentage, how likely are you to steal if you thought you wouldn't be caught?*
> ( ) *0–10%*
> ( ) *10–30%*

( ) *30–60%*
( ) *60–80%*
( ) *90–100%*

Being realistic counts against you almost as much as being honest. If you are aware of how the world works, then your innocence is lost and you are therefore corrupt . . . or at least corruptible. It's flawed logic to be sure. Being aware of the murder rate doesn't make you Jack the Ripper, but remember, it's all about making the bigwigs feel better.

Once you understand the real subtext of a personality test question, it becomes a lot easier to answer. On the next page are sample personality test questions. Below each question is the true subtext in *italics*. Answer the questions honestly and realistically, then compare your answer to the subtext version to see how you did.

Sample Personality Test

1. Have you ever told a lie during your lifetime?
( ) Yes
( ) No

1. Are you a liar?
( ) *Yes*
( ) *No*

2. Supervisors need to monitor their employees carefully if they expect them to be productive.
( ) Completely agree
( ) Mostly agree
( ) Mostly disagree
( ) Completely disagree

2. Do you slack off when unsupervised?
( ) *Always*
( ) *Usually*
( ) *Sometimes*
( ) *No*

3. What percentage of people do you think regularly take longer breaks than they are supposed to?
( ) 0–20%
( ) 20–40%
( ) 40–60%
( ) 60–80%
( ) 80–100%

3. *How often will you commit payroll fraud?*
( ) *Never*
( ) *Infrequently*
( ) *Often*
( ) *A lot*
( ) *Every time I go on break*

4. What is the largest amount of money you have ever stolen?
( ) $1–$10
( ) $10–$50
( ) $50–$100
( ) $100–$1,000
( ) $1000+
( ) I've never stolen anything

4. *Are you a thief?*
( ) *Yes*
( ) *Yes*
( ) *Yes*
( ) *Yes*
( ) *Big time*
( ) *No*

5. Do you always obey the posted speed limit?
( ) Always
( ) Usually
( ) Seldom
( ) Never

5. How often do you blatantly disregard the law?
( ) *Never*
( ) *Seldom*
( ) *Usually*
( ) *Always*

6. Have you ever talked about someone behind his or her back?
( ) No
( ) Yes, but only once or twice
( ) Yes, often

6. Are you going to corrupt other employees with your bad attitude?
( ) *No*
( ) *Only if you really make me angry*
( ) *I poison minds as a hobby*

7. Have you ever lied to spare someone's feelings?
( ) Yes
( ) No

7. Are you too weak to tell it like it is?
( ) *Yes*
( ) *No*

8. Jon and Frank are discussing a coworker who was dismissed.

> JON: Did you hear? Greg got fired for stealing CDs.
> FRANK: Really? That sucks! Greg was cool. I don't blame him at all for taking stuff. He only makes minimum wage and he gets treated like dirt!
> JON: Well, that may be so, but stealing is wrong. Greg had no right to do that.

( ) I agree with Jon
( ) I agree with Jon, but Frank has a point

( ) I agree with both Jon and Frank
( ) I agree with Frank, but Jon has a point
( ) I agree with Frank

*8. Jon and Frank are discussing a coworker who
was dismissed.*

> *JON: Did you hear? Greg got fired for stealing CDs.*
> *FRANK: Really? Well, I'm an immoral jerk who thinks
> stealing is fine and dandy!*
> *JON: Well, I'm not. I follow the straight and
> narrow.*

( ) *I follow the straight and narrow, too*
( ) *I try to be good, but I have bad thoughts*
( ) *I can't make moral decisions—I'm a sheep*
( ) *I'm fairly evil, but my annoying conscience
nags at me sometimes*
( ) *I'm the scum of the earth*

9. You are waiting at the bus stop when you see a man
drop a $10 bill. Before you can say anything, he gets on
the bus and it speeds away. What do you do?
( ) Pocket the money
( ) Ignore it—let someone else pick it up
( ) Give it to the homeless
( ) Give it to the police with a description of the man
and the bus number

*9. Do you capitalize on the misfortune of others when
there is no fear of retribution?*
( ) *Absolutely*
( ) *No, but I'm still too lazy to do the right thing*
( ) *Yes, but I do it Robin Hood–style to avoid feeling
guilty*
( ) *No, I do the right thing even when I know my
efforts will be wasted*

10. A coworker that you strongly dislike forgets to claim the commission from a sale. What would you do?
( ) I would tell him about the sale he missed
( ) I wouldn't say anything. Let him figure it out. That's his problem.
( ) I would claim the sale and commission for myself

10. Are you vindictive?
( ) *No*
( ) *Yes, but only in a passive/aggressive sort of way*
( ) *Cross me and I will make it my sole purpose in life to take you down*

How'd you do? Well, hopefully you now see the value of lying on the test. You may think it's absurd to claim you have never told a lie, but I've seen people fail these tests because they answered one too many questions like a normal human being.

Ironically, these tests not only encourage the very dishonesty they are trying to weed out, but favor the most brazen liars who are willing to tell you the most implausible things to get hired. Personally, I wouldn't hire anyone who got 100 percent on this test . . . but they would, so be sure to lay it on thick.

An Alternative Personality Test

While the existing personality tests are obviously flawed, the idea of testing prospective employees in order to predetermine their suitability as retail workers is an intriguing one. So I've designed my own personality test to determine whether you are suited to work in retail.

I recommend taking this test before continuing—especially if you've never worked in retail before.

The Official Retail Employee Handbook Personality Test

1. Is your faith in humanity easily shaken?
( ) No. It takes an utterly abominable act like genocide to make me question the nature of man.

( ) Somewhat. The nightly news often tests my faith
    in people.
( ) Yes. When someone tries to buy cigarettes with food
    stamps, I add another page to my manifesto.

2. How attached are you to your dignity?
( ) Very. It's the one thing I insist on keeping, no matter
    what the situation.
( ) Somewhat. It's important to me, but I try to have a
    sense of humor about it.
( ) Not at all. I'm more than happy to dress up in a
    humiliating costume and wave at cars in 100-degree
    heat for minimum wage. The costume is dirty, too?
    Not a problem.

3. Under which conditions would you expect the mall to
close early?
( ) A blizzard
( ) A hurricane
( ) A tornado
( ) The apocalypse
( ) None of the above

4. How do you prefer to be addressed?
( ) Sir/Ma'am. I demand an air of respect.
( ) Mr./Mrs./Miss. I expect some degree of professionalism.
( ) First name is fine. I don't have any ego hang-ups.
( ) "Hey you!" or a curt whistle will suffice.

5. How much abuse can you tolerate?
( ) None. Abuse should never be tolerated.
( ) Not much. I'll make it clear when you've crossed
    the line.
( ) A fair amount. I have a pretty high boiling point.
( ) A lot. My skin is so thick from being mistreated,
    I'm bulletproof.

6. How do you typically deal with someone who you feel is being unreasonable?
( ) With patience and understanding
( ) With a firm hand and straight talk
( ) With an AK-47

7. Which of the ten federal holidays do you expect to have off? Check all that apply.
( ) Thanksgiving
( ) Christmas Day

8. What type of health care are you accustomed to?
( ) HMO
( ) PPO
( ) A first-aid kit and a wish

9. Which of the following retirement plans do you find the most realistic?
( ) 401(k)
( ) Social security
( ) Online Texas Hold 'em

10. Pertaining to customers, which philosophy do you agree with the most?
( ) The customer is always right
( ) There's a sucker born every minute
( ) Live and let die

To receive your official "Retail" suitability quotient by e-mail, visit www.NormanFeuti.com and submit your answers.

CHAPTER **4**

Training

Hopefully you've followed my advice up to this point and have landed a tolerable retail job. Congratulations! Now let's get you ready for your first big day.

Your entire first day will be consumed by training, but don't expect to learn much during this process. Training new employees costs money, and since retailers suffer a whopping 33-percent turnover rate on average, the constant influx of new employees turns into a huge expense. In an attempt to cut the cost of training new employees, retailers cram as much information as they can into booklets, videos, and tests—essentially leaving it up to the new recruits to train themselves.

While this technique does indeed save money, the lack of hands-on training fosters a general sense of apathy and dissatisfaction in the employees that only serves to perpetuate the high turnover rate that is so costly in the first place.

But none of that is your problem. Here are some tips on how to get through the training process. These tips apply to most retail jobs, so you should be able to use them again when you find work at a different store about eighteen months from now.

Note: Some rogue managers will skip the protocols handed down from corporate in favor of their own "sink or swim" approach to training. If you're unlucky enough to get one of these renegade managers, you'll be given a ten-minute crash course on the register, then be left to fend for yourself. If that happens, you'll be glad you bought this book.

PRETENDING TO READ THE HANDBOOK

After you've filled out the obligatory W-4 and I-9 forms, you'll be given an employee handbook to read and sign off on. Some handbooks are short, some are long, but they all contain the same basic rules and statements.

You won't be quizzed on this stuff later, so you don't really have to read the handbook. Its only real function is to provide your employer with legal protection. They couldn't care less if you're informed, just as long as you sign away any future claim to ignorance of the rules.

Pretending to read the handbook is a good time to be alone with your thoughts or maybe poke through the manager's desk. Just be sure to turn to a new section of the book every few minutes in case another employee passes through. When you get to the last page, just sit there until your supervisor comes in to check on you, then act as though you just finished and sign off on it. Your supervisor will be happy about the perfect timing and move you on to the next step in your training.

The Handbook in a Nutshell

If you've never read an employee handbook before, you might be curious about its contents. To save you the trouble of reading the real thing, I'll give you some of the highlights. Unlike the text in the average handbook, I'll dispense with the pleasantries and get straight to each point.

We Are an Equal Opportunity Employer
WE'RE NOT BIGOTS

We are not bigots. If any of the people working for us are bigots, we don't know about it. If we find out that you're discriminating against customers or other employees based on race, religion, gender, or sexual orientation, don't expect sensitivity training—we'll just fire you. We don't have time for that crap.

If you're the victim of discrimination by another employee, please don't call the ACLU. Call our human resources department instead. We'll handle it for you. We promise.

Zero-Tolerance Sexual Harassment Policy
NO PERVERTS

We don't care who you are or how things work in your neck of the woods. If we catch you doing anything that can be construed as inappropriate, we're not going to ignore it or sweep it under the rug like we used to. Nowadays, we can get sued over your sophomoric behavior, so knock it off!

Like discrimination, if you're the victim of sexual harassment by another employee, call HR. There's no need to get the authorities involved. Please let us take care of it. We're begging you.

Drug-and-Alcohol-Free Environment
GET HIGH ON YOUR OWN TIME

It's sad that we have to tell you this, but you can't come to work drunk or stoned. Believe it or not, snorting a few rails of coke isn't the best prelude to great customer service. Don't even think about bringing your junk to work either. We won't hesitate to narc on you if we find your stash in the break room. Having you arrested is much easier than firing you.

You've been warned. Let's move on.

No Firearms and Other Weapons
LEAVE YOUR PSYCHO TOYS AT HOME

If you show up to work with a pair of nunchucks or the longsword you bought at the local renaissance festival, we're going to seriously reconsider our decision to employ you. If you show up to work with a loaded Colt .45 in your waistband, we're going to call the SWAT team to take you out. If you're lucky, you'll only be tackled and beaten instead of riddled with bullets.

Progressive Discipline Policy
HOW WE GO ABOUT FIRING YOU

If you screw up in some huge way, your dismissal will be fairly succinct. But if you turn out to be a plain old slacker, the procedure is a little different. In order to avoid paying unemployment benefits to layabouts, we have to document their laziness. If you're going to get fired for this reason, we'll give you a couple of written warnings beforehand, so you'll see it coming.

Employee Stock Purchase Program
THE DISCOUNT YOU WON'T BE USING

We offer our employees a discount on stocks. Of course, we barely pay you enough money to live on, so we doubt that you have a lot of spare cash to invest. Even if you did, you wouldn't be likely to invest it here, since you know how the place works and all. But just so you know.

Health Benefits
TRY NOT TO GET SICK

Unless you're a manager, we're not going to give you enough hours to qualify as a full-time employee. That way we're not required to give you the health benefits we offer our employees in the corporate office. So if you're not a manager, try not to get sick.

If you are a manager, try not to get sick either. We want to keep our premiums down.

Vacation Time
TWO WEEKS OF FREEDOM

Only full-time employees are eligible for paid vacation, and we already covered the fact that there are no non-management full-timers. If you non-managers ask us really nicely at least five weeks in advance, we'll graciously allow you to take some unpaid vacation time. We probably won't even replace you while you're gone.

As for the managers, you start off with two weeks of paid vacation every year. Theoretically, you accrue more vacation time the longer you work for us, but we've never seen that happen. Just remember, you can't take your two weeks of vacation consecutively or anywhere near each other. You're also not allowed to take any vacation time in November, December, or January. Not that you could afford to go anywhere tropical anyway.

Military and Jury Duty
THE GOVERNMENT IS MORE POWERFUL THAN US

If we could avoid the costs associated with allowing you to fulfill your civic obligations or military duties, we would. Unfortunately we haven't figured out how to get around those laws yet.

"At Will" Employment
YOU HAVE NO JOB SECURITY

Let's call it like it is. You don't care about us and we don't care about you. At the end of the day, we're both going to do whatever we need to do to get by. If you find a better job, you'll leave us high and dry. If our gross mismanagement forces us to close your store, you're out on the street. We don't owe each other anything.

TRAINING VIDEOS: A LAUGH RIOT!

At some point you will be made to watch a bunch of training videos. Most stores have a single TV/VCR unit on a little cart in the break room for just this purpose. You might notice a twisted-up coat hanger and/or a beat-up videotape sleeve for *Die Hard* or *Gremlins* on the cart. Just ignore them for now, we'll cover that in Chapter 9: Break Time.

While the subject matter of the videos you have to watch will vary from store to store, you can count on them all to be *hilarious*. Of course they won't be intentionally funny. They'll be funny in the way a really bad movie is funny—*Mystery Science Theater 3000* funny, if you will. So sit back and enjoy, but try not to laugh out loud. You don't want to be pegged as someone with a bad attitude right off the bat.

The bad acting and generally poor production standards are comedy gold all by themselves, but the funniest aspect of any training video is the pretense that it reflects anything even remotely resembling reality. In the video world, well-groomed customers interact happily with knowledgable salespeople in immaculate stores. The sales techniques work like magic, everyone does what they're supposed to, and the system works.

I've often wondered if the people in the corporate office actually believe their training videos depict reality, or if they recognize them as pure propaganda. I could honestly see it both ways.

Keeping It Real

If I were to produce a retail training video, I would do things differently. I suppose if I were a soulless yes-man corporate type, I'd still have to make the video comply with whatever lame philosophy the company wanted me to push, but I wouldn't sugarcoat things. I would at least create a somewhat believable retail world so the employees would come away from it with realistic expectations about the environment they're about to enter.

I think it would go something like this:

The Grumbel's G.U.E.S.T. Treatment!

A video screenplay by:

Norman Feuti

FADE IN:

INTERIOR—GRUMBEL'S DEPARTMENT STORE—
SALES FLOOR

In the background grumpy shoppers mill about,
carelessly displacing merchandise and knocking over
fixtures. LAURA, a perky twenty-something
saleswoman, enters the foreground and smiles at the
camera, seemingly unaware of the mess the patrons
are making.

LAURA

(cheerfully)

Hi, and welcome to Grumbel's! I'm Laura and
I'm going to be your guide to great service! In
this video, you'll learn all about the Grumbel's
G.U.E.S.T. treatment—our tried-and-true method
of exceeding the expectations of happy shoppers
throughout the world. Come on, let's get started!

Laura walks out of shot, playfully beckoning the
viewer to follow. In the background shoppers continue

wrecking the place. A teenage girl sticks a wad of gum
under a display table. A man casually tosses a drink cup
over his shoulder.

CUT TO:

INTERIOR—GRUMBEL'S—STOCKROOM

Boxes are everywhere. They are packed to the
ceiling on overcrowded shelves, heaped onto dollies,
and haphazardly stacked on the floor. LAURA stumbles
past a pile of boxes into the shot, almost falling.

               LAURA
            (apologetically)
Whoa! Sorry about the mess, we're a little
shorthanded at the moment.

LAURA straightens her clothing and puts on her best
smile.

               LAURA
             (coyly)
Before we let you back onto the sales floor,
I need to fill you in on a little secret. Did you
know that Grumbel's doesn't have any
customers?

LAURA pauses, then laughs.

               LAURA
            (rolls eyes)
Don't worry. We're not going out of business.
Grumbel's doesn't have any customers because
we don't call them customers. We call them
guests!

SUPERIMPOSE: G.U.E.S.T.

>   LAURA
> We call our patrons guests because it helps us to
> remember how we should treat each and every
> person who comes through our doors—like a
> guest in our own home!

LAURA flourishes a hand over the superimposed letters.

>   LAURA
> G.-U.-E.-S.-T. is also an acronym that helps us
> remember five very important steps we must
> follow when helping each cust . . . I mean guest.

CUT TO:

INTERIOR—GRUMBEL'S—MALL ENTRANCE

A gruff-looking middle-aged man enters the store.
AMANDA, a young female employee, straightens a
nearby rack of clothing.

SUPERIMPOSE: Greet

>   LAURA
>   (voiceover)
> The G in G.U.E.S.T. stands for "greet." Warmly
> greeting each person who visits our store makes
> them feel welcome and lets them know you are
> ready to help them if they need it. Watch our ace
> greeter, Amanda, in action!

>   AMANDA
>   (enthusiastically)
> Hi, how are you today?

GRUFF MAN
(annoyed/angry)
I'm just looking. Can't I just look?!

AMANDA goes back to her work perturbed.

LAURA (voiceover)
See? It's just that easy!

CUT TO:

INTERIOR—GRUMBEL'S—ELECTRONICS DEPARTMENT

A woman stands near a display of computers. DOUG, a young salesman, approaches her to ask if she needs help.

SUPERIMPOSE: Understand

LAURA (voiceover)
The U in G.U.E.S.T. stands for "understand."
When you help a guest, be sure to ask them
leading questions so you can truly understand
their needs. Here's Doug to show you how it's
done.

DOUG
Hi, is there anything I can help you find?

WOMAN
Well, I'm looking for a computer, but I don't know
what to get.

DOUG
Okay, what are you planning on using it for?

WOMAN
(suspiciously)
Why do you need to know that?

DOUG
(apologetically)
Oh, I don't mean to pry, it will just help me guide
you to the right kind of computer. Do you want
it mostly for word processing or graphic work?
Do you just want to surf the Web?

WOMAN
(snottily)
Don't you have a computer that can do all of that?

DOUG
Um, well, yes. This iMac comes with a ton of
software and is an extremely versatile . . .

WOMAN
(interrupting/accusatory)
That's twice as expensive as the others! You're
just trying to sell me the one that costs the most
money!

DOUG
(irritated)
You said you wanted one that can do everything!
If you would be more specific about what you
want, I'd be able to recommend a cheaper model.
I don't care which one you buy!

WOMAN
(indignantly)
I don't think you know what you're talking about!

The woman storms off, while DOUG clenches his teeth
and balls his fists, trying hard to contain his rage.

LAURA (voiceover)
(sympathetically)
Oh, well. Better luck next time, Doug!

CUT TO:

INTERIOR—GRUMBEL'S—MEN'S SHOE DEPARTMENT

PHIL, a neatly dressed salesman, waits on a man who
is trying on dress shoes.

SUPERIMPOSE: Explain

LAURA (voiceover)
The E in G.U.E.S.T. stands for "explain." Remember
to always explain the features and benefits of a
product. When you take the time to educate the
guest, he or she will feel more comfortable making
a purchase. Watch how Phil puts his product
knowledge to good use.

MAN
(trying on shoes)
I don't know, they feel all right, but they're kind
of expensive.

PHIL
(reassuring)
It's a high-quality dress shoe, sir. It's 100-percent
leather, has a steel shank and a welted sole
construction. So it's a very durable shoe that will
last you a long time.

MAN
(sits down in chair)
Don't you have any sales going on?

PHIL
(politely sympathetic)
No, not on those. Our top-of-the-line dress shoes
rarely go on sale.

MAN
(whining)
They're just so expensive.

PHIL
Well, you get what you pay for.

MAN
(bitterly)
Humph. Not always.

Long pause.

MAN
You don't have any coupons? Anything?

PHIL
No, sorry.

Long pause.

MAN
There's nothing you can do to knock a few bucks
off? Not even like ten dollars?

                        PHIL
                      (bluntly)
        No, I have no control over the prices.

The man looks down at the shoes and sighs heavily,
but says nothing.

                        PHIL
        Uh, would you like to try something else on?

                        MAN
              (pouting/looking at shoes)
                  Give me a minute.
PHIL's eyes begin to glaze over as he waits for
the man to make a decision. The man just sits
motionless, looking broodingly at the new shoes
on his feet.

                 LAURA (voiceover)
        Um, we'll check back in on Phil a little later.

CUT TO:

INTERIOR—GRUMBEL'S—CHECKOUT COUNTER

A woman approaches the checkout counter carrying
three small vases. CLAIRE, the girl behind the counter,
turns to help her.

SUPERIMPOSE: Sell

                 LAURA (voiceover)
        The S in G.U.E.S.T. stands for "sell." Making the
        sale is what it's all about, so you should do
        whatever it takes to make it happen. Watch how
        CLAIRE goes out of her way to make a sale.

WOMAN
(places three vases on counter)
Excuse me, you only have three of these vases
in stock, but I need thirty of them for a wedding
shower I'm throwing. Can I order them?

CLAIRE
(looks at vases warily)
Ooh, those are discontinued, so we can't order
them anymore. Let me call the Grumbel's in the
next town over to see if they have any.

WOMAN
Thank you.
CLAIRE phones another store with no luck.

CLAIRE
(apologetically)
I'm sorry, they didn't have any.

WOMAN
Well, I really want them, so can you call
every other store on the east coast right now to see
if you can scrounge together all thirty? I'll wait.

CLAIRE
(sarcastically)
Yeah, I've got nothing better to do.

CLAIRE begrudgingly picks up the phone, flips open a
large binder marked "Store Directory," and begins
dialing.

LAURA (voiceover)
(enthusiastically)
Way to go, Claire!

CUT TO:

INTERIOR—GRUMBEL'S—CHECKOUT COUNTER

JENNIFER the cashier finishes ringing up a sale with
the same gruff middle-aged man who entered the store
from the mall earlier.

SUPERIMPOSE: Thank

> LAURA (voiceover)
> And finally, the T in G.U.E.S.T. stands for, "thank."
> Be sure to let every guest know how much we
> appreciate them with a simple thank-you.

JENNIFER puts a receipt in the gruff man's shopping
bag and hands it to him.

> JENNIFER
> (smiling warmly)
> Thank you for shopping at Grumbel's! Have a
> great afternoon!

The gruff man snatches the bag quickly and trudges
off without so much as making eye contact. JENNIFER
immediately loses her pleasant demeanor at this snub
and flips out.

> JENNIFER
> (shouting angrily)
> I'll have a nice day, too, you jerk! You want a
> piece of me?! Come back here!!!

CUT TO:

INTERIOR—GRUMBEL'S—ORIGINAL SALES FLOOR SHOT

LAURA stands smiling in the foreground. AMANDA, DOUG, PHIL, CLAIRE, and JENNIFER all stand behind her looking absolutely miserable. There are no longer customers in the background, but the store is a complete mess.

> LAURA
> (cheerily)
> There you have it—the Grumbel's G.U.E.S.T. treatment! I hope you've found this video both instructional and enlightening. And remember, even if you think the five steps are ineffective, you have to do them anyway. You have no choice.

AMANDA, DOUG, PHIL, CLAIRE, and JENNIFER all slump visibly at the grim reality of what LAURA has said.

> LAURA
> (still cheery)
> So long for now and happy selling!

LAURA waves enthusiastically, while the others remain slumped and downtrodden.

FADE TO BLACK

THE CASH REGISTER

In spite of what any retailer might say about priding oneself on product knowledge or great service, the emphasis of your training is going to be on the cash register. In fact, learning how to use the register is so important to retailers that they will actually have a real person train you how to use it. Some places even have a computer simulator to pre-train you before the real person trains you. That's how much they care.

Modern-day cash registers are not without their problems, but using them is easy compared to the cast-iron tills of yesteryear. Just ask anyone over fifty who worked in retail back in the day and they'll tell you how much the old-timey registers and inventory systems used to suck. I have nothing but respect for anyone who worked in the dark ages of retail, when everything was handwritten and the register was little more than a drawer to keep the money in.

But it's not the operation of the register that will be challenging—they'll hold your hand through that process. What's going to be difficult is learning how to deal with the ineptitude, deviousness, and general rude behavior of the people you'll be ringing up. Coping with that is something they won't teach you. You'll be left to figure that out all on your own.

Luckily you have this handbook. I'll give you a crash course in how to deal with some of the more common annoyances you will face while running the register.

"It Must Be Free!"

Often, a customer will hand you a product with no price tag, or a barcode that won't scan, and you'll have to call someone to do a price check or punch in the UPC manually. When this happens, you have to be ready.

Anytime the price of a product cannot be instantly ascertained for any reason, there is an 87-percent chance that the customer will quip, "It must be free!" During the course of any given day, you should expect to hear this "joke" an average of three times.

Never reward this witticism with a fake laugh. This will only encourage the customer to use this lame joke again and again at other stores. The only way the "it must be free" joke can be eradicated is if all retail employees unite in shooting it down with an icy glare every time they hear it. If every customer was made to feel horribly uncomfortable whenever they said it, the joke would eventually die out.

If you're not part of the solution on this one, you're part of the problem.

Cutting in Line

You would think the grade-school act of cutting in line wouldn't be a problem in the world of adults, but it is. Most commonly, cutting happens when a new register opens up and the cashier says, "I can help the *next* person in line." Then a person who is clearly not the next person in line rushes to the new register.

There are two distinct camps on how to respond when this happens. The first camp feels the cutter should be called on his or her shenanigans and sent to the back of the line. The second camp couldn't give a rat's ass.

I personally fall into the second camp. It's not that I think the cutter should get away with it, I just don't feel that I'm obligated to speak up on behalf of the other able-bodied adults in line. If they don't stand up for themselves, then that's their problem.

You'll have to decide for yourself what camp you're in, but let me educate you on the dangers inherent to both camps.

Camp One

If you take it upon yourself to call someone on cutting, you run the risk of a confrontation. The cutter might outright refuse to give up his or her newly acquired place in line. When this happens, you'll find that the customers you so valiantly stood up for will fall silent. They won't want to be involved in a face-off, so they suddenly won't care that they were cut, leaving you to deal with an awkward situation all by yourself.

Only under extreme circumstances would I recommend taking the camp one approach. I wouldn't risk the hassle unless the person being cut was clearly worthy of being defended— like someone in a wheelchair, or a little kid . . . or a really hot chick.

Camp Two

Ignoring the cutter is usually the way to go, but it's not without its dangers. When you clearly let someone get away with cutting, you run the risk of angering the other people in line. If this happens, you'll be viewed as an accomplice and the people in line will take their anger out on you.

You can avoid that by using a simple technique I've developed. Whenever you have to go to your register, do *not* look at the other lines as you approach. Go directly to the register and say, "I can help the next person in line," but keep your eyes glued to the floor until someone gets to your counter. If the person happens to be a cutter, anyone watching will observe that you didn't see the cut happen. This way the worst you can be accused of is not paying attention.

Ignorance is bliss.

Cell Phone Rudeness

Nothing irks me more than ringing up a customer who is talking on their cell phone. It's just common courtesy to acknowledge the person who is handling your purchase and bagging your stuff. I can't count the number of times my salutations have been completely ignored by someone talking on the phone. I once rang up a woman who was simultaneously writing out a check and talking on the phone. Here's how it went down:

The lady brought her items to my register while talking on her cell phone.

ME: Hi, how are you?

She dropped her items on the counter and completely ignored me. I rang her up and bagged the items.

> ME: That'll be $33.92.

She took out her checkbook and started writing one out. She continued talking on the phone as she did so. When she needed to fill in the amount she stopped.

> LADY: How much was that?
> ME: $33.92.

As I repeated the amount, she became distracted by her phone conversation. She bolted upright and put a hand on her hip.

> LADY: [On phone] You're kidding me. Oh, my God!

The man behind her in line was clearly becoming impatient.

> LADY: [To me] I'm sorry, how much?
> ME: $33.92.

She was about to write it down, but again became distracted by her phone call.

> LADY: [To phone] What? No way? I totally cannot believe that!
> MAN BEHIND HER: Come on!

She didn't hear him. She talked for a few more seconds before getting back to the check.

> LADY: [To me] Sorry, *how* much?

I just twisted the price display toward her so she could read it herself.

MAN BEHIND HER: *Sigh*. Unbelievable!

She finally wrote the amount down and I finished the transaction. I handed her the receipt.

ME: Have a nice day.

Still talking on the phone and ignoring me, she grabbed the receipt and left . . . without her merchandise.

The story would be better if she never came back, but she did. A few moments later, she came back in still talking on the phone. She grabbed her bag from the counter and shot me a nasty look as if it was my fault that she forgot it.

There's a certain class of people who think the world is their own personal space, so there's no getting around the frequent rudeness associated with cell phones. But instead of getting angry, get even. While the customer chats away, feel free to double ring an item, or neglect removing the security tag from their purchase—anything that is easy to fix and can be pawned off as an accident. The inconvenience it causes them will teach them a valuable lesson about keeping alert.

Card Swiping

Most registers come equipped with a keypad that customers can use to swipe their own debit card and punch in their PIN. It's commonplace technology, yet many people have still not mastered the art of using these devices. In spite of the ubiquitous graphic that illustrates how the card should be swiped, some people still manage to swipe the card the incorrect way, repeatedly.

Even if you ignore the illustration, there are only eight possible ways to run a rectangular card through a narrow slot. But some customers seem to be able to beat all statistical probability by randomly swiping their card the same seven wrong ways over and over again.

This will go on forever if you let it, so when you get one of these customers, be firm and set limits. Each customer gets three chances to get it right. After that, you have to take their card and swipe it for them. Don't ask or try to instruct them, it will just make things more aggravating. Just grab the card and do it.

My Pen!

Do yourself a favor. Hide a package of pens somewhere near the registers and don't tell anyone about them. Coworkers and customers alike will walk off with the pens from your register on a regular basis, so it's a good idea to have an emergency stash.

A good percentage of the transactions you'll handle on the register will require a pen, so suddenly finding yourself without one is not good. Without a pen, you are one credit-card purchase away from being completely helpless. There's no worse feeling then being isolated on the register with no pen.

Forget about calling for help. When there's a pen shortage, you're on your own. The other cashiers will quickly take on a depression-era dustbowl mentality and turn their backs on you. *"I got my own slips to worry about! I can't help you!"*

Don't let this happen to you.

CHAPTER **5**

Your Coworkers

Y ou have the job and you've made it through the training process. Now it's time to get to know the diverse group of people you're going to be working with.

Many consumers like to think that all retail workers come from the bottom of the barrel. They think that every store clerk is a lazy, uneducated moron unfit to hold a "real job." But the reality is that there is no greater percentage of idiots working in retail than in any other job. The only difference between Wal-Mart and IBM is that the general public doesn't witness the occasional screwups and shiftlessness of the IBM employees. If you were allowed to walk into any office in the country and observe the work ethic, you'd find just as many slackers there as you would in the average store. Non-retail workers wouldn't be so quick to judge if they had customers walking through their cubicles at random, treating them like complete losers whenever they got caught surfing the Internet.

"Excuse me! I hate to interrupt your leisure time, but I'd like a little service!"

The idea that retail employees are all uneducated is also unfounded, especially since a high percentage of store clerks and cashiers are working their way through college. It's always a rending experience to watch a coworker with a BA in English get rebuked by some palooka who barely made it through high school.

"Whatcha mean ya ain't got my brand of cigarettes?! Didn't ya order enough, stupid?!"

I'm not trying to tell you that everyone you work with in retail is going to be the salt of the earth—far from it. I'm just trying to dispel the stereotype. Every workplace has both good and bad employees and retail is no different.

BEING THE NEWBIE

Like any new job, you have to pay your dues. The transition from newbie to trusted colleague is a slow process, so you should count on being handed the crappiest jobs the store has to offer for at least the first month. Everyone has to go through an initiation period, so when they tell you to clean the toilets or climb into the cardboard compactor when it gets jammed, just suck it up. You can't be accepted into the flock until you've felt their pain.

On top of the crappy jobs you'll have to do during your initiation, your coworkers will also play pranks on you. Don't take it personally. You're being tested to see how much abuse you can tolerate. If you can't take a little good-natured humiliation, you'll never survive what the customers can dish out, so lighten up.

But since this book is meant to give you a leg up on the rest, I'll let you in on a classic retail gag that is often played on newbies. It's called the "wall-stretcher."

The Wall-Stretcher

The premise of this joke is simple. A newbie is nonchalantly asked by a coworker to go in the back and get the "wall-stretcher." The name should be a dead giveaway that this device is completely fictitious, but the rookie will usually embark on a lengthy and frustrating search for it without question. Of course, no one assumes that a tool exists that can literally stretch walls by magically extending matter; most people just figure the name is meant in some colloquial way. Not wanting to look stupid, the newbie will set off hoping that he'll know the device when he sees it, or that it will be clearly marked.

Eventually the rookie gives up and his coworkers will let him in on the joke, revealing that they were watching the futile search and mocking his diligence the whole time. The joke becomes even more priceless/humiliating when the pigeon actually comes back with some odd tool or shelf bracket thinking he's found it.

If anyone tries to make you the victim of the wall-stretcher bit, you can play it one of two ways.

1) You can let them know you're in on the joke. They'll be disappointed, but they'll also respect how retail savvy you are.
2) You can play dumb and disappear for a while. If you work in a mall or shopping center, the joke might involve sending you to other stores that may have "borrowed" the fictitious device, in which case you've really lucked out and can go shopping. Who's the sucker now?

Note: There is a similar prank common to shoe stores. Instead of the wall-stretcher they send you out looking for the "shoelace-repair kit."

THE ARCHETYPES

Although there is no stereotypical retail employee, there are twelve basic archetypes that most of your coworkers will fit into. It's important to identify them quickly so you know whom to make friends with and whom to avoid.

Animosity Generator (AG)

Of all the retail employees, the animosity generator is the most loathsome. There is always at least one AG in every retail establishment. True to their name, animosity generators are employees who are so outwardly rude, socially inept, lazy, and unhelpful that they are predominantly responsible for the negative stereotype that all retail workers suffer from. If someone prejudges you as a retail employee, it's probably because they've had a recent run-in with an AG. Maybe some bastard carelessly jammed a two-liter bottle of Pepsi and a jar of pickles on top of their eggs the last time they went grocery shopping—who knows?

On top of being responsible for the majority of the bad feelings toward retail workers, AGs are so incompetent and uncaring that they screw up every job given to them. Nothing bites worse than having to undo, and then redo, some task that has been completely mucked up by an AG. Some animosity generators actually screw up on purpose to discourage their superiors from ever asking them to do anything, but most of them are just stupid.

It goes without saying that you should avoid animosity generators like the plague. If you ever have any designs on attempting to get the AG where you work fired, forget about it. In spite of their gross ineptitude, animosity generators are mysteriously immune to disciplinary action or termination.

Artist

Whether they be musicians, writers, illustrators, photographers, actors, or graphic designers, there are a ton of artists working in retail. Many theories abound as to why so many artists flock to retail, but the most prevalently accepted reason is that they thrive on discontent. The daily inequities and reprehensible nature of retail work serve as fuel for many modern-day bohemians. Suffering and art go hand in hand.

It's always good to know a couple of artists. They love to have a good time and aren't afraid to party. If you want to know where the best clubs are, ask an artist. But keep the appearance of your relationship with any artist at work distant. Artists have a notoriously low tolerance for bullshit, so they're bound to flip off the boss and walk out one day. When that happens, you don't want it to look as if the two of you were best buds.

Curmudgeon

Not to be confused with the animosity generator, curmudgeons are outwardly rude, socially inept, and unhelpful not because they were born that way, but because they have been made that way through years of abuse. During their tenure in retail, curmudgeons have discovered that customers will abuse you regardless of your attitude, so they have decided to abandon niceties altogether. Curmudgeons are also responsible for much of the bad feeling toward retail employees, because they are indiscriminate in their rudeness. They treat every customer like scum. If you politely ask a sales clerk where the shampoo is and they curtly answer, *"That's not my department!"* you're dealing with a curmudgeon.

Ironically, this attitude actually creates more of the very customer conflicts and complaints that made the curmudgeon the way he or she is in the first place. This pointless circle of hate can continue for years before the curmudgeon finally burns out.

Like AGs, curmudgeons should be avoided.

Devil's Advocate (DA)

The devil's advocate is a real pain in the ass. Whenever you've had a bad day and need to vent about the job or the customers, a DA will delight in defending the object of your scorn. Devil's advocates love to say stuff like, *"You take things too personally,"* or *"The company has to do what's best for business."* No matter how extreme the situation you've had to deal with, a DA will criticize you for being angry and will be sure to tell you how they would have handled it better. If a customer took a dump on your head, a devil's advocate would find a way to justify it.

"Well you know, our restrooms really should be closer to the front of the store. The customers can't be expected to hold it that long."

Outside of just hauling off and punching him or her in the face, the best way to deal with a devil's advocate is by being patient. Eventually the DA himself will fall victim to some extraspecial retail bullshit, and then you can return the favor. Payback's a bitch.

Geek

While it would be tedious to list every personality type that could work in retail, the geek deserves mention. Geeks can work anywhere, but usually end up working around their interests and obsessions. Geeks are most often encountered anywhere books, computers, video games, and toys are sold.

Despite their obvious social foibles, geeks are good to know because of their encyclopedic knowledge of the merchandise. Sooner or later, someone is going to want to know something about the products you sell, so having a geek as a buddy you can turn to is very useful.

To maintain the friendship, you might have to endure the occasional dissertation on *Lord of the Rings* characters, but it's worth it.

Jerk

The one universal truth about jerks is that they have a constant need to feel better about themselves and they accomplish this by trying to make other people feel stupid or inferior. I've heard a lot of theories on how to best deal with jerks, but in my experience the most effective way is to make fun of them behind their backs.

The cathartic effect of cutting someone down on a regular basis is almost worth the abuse to begin with. When everyone sits around the break room and joins in on hating someone who deserves every bit of that ire, it's like sweet music. In the end, you feel better, you get to bond with the other coworkers, and you can't wait until the next outrageous thing the jerk does so you can hate on him or her all over again.

Lifer

Lifers are retail veterans who are destined to spend the rest of their days working behind the counter. Unlike the curmudgeon, the lifer has attained a state of retail Zen in their countless years of experience, acknowledging the paradoxical nature of their job and transcending rational thought. There's nothing they haven't seen, so nothing shocks or bothers them anymore. Lifers are numb to the horrors of retail much like a coroner is numb to the sight of a cadaver.

Lifers know how to work the system, so it's wise to stay on good terms with them. Whenever you need to know how things work or what you can get away with, just ask a lifer.

Slacker

Everyone slacks from time to time, but the true slacker has turned it into an art form. Slackers are masters of goofing off while appearing to be busy, and have the ability to hide from the boss or customers like a ninja.

Many people are under the misconception that slackers are lazy, when actually the opposite is true. Slackers are extremely fast and competent workers who simply don't want to be punished for their efficiency by having to do more work than is expected of others. If running ten boxes of stock takes the average employee two hours to complete, then the slacker thinks he should get two hours to do the job as well. When the job only takes the slacker thirty minutes, he just figures he should get to spend the other hour and a half any way he pleases.

Employees who slack a lot but don't get their work done are not true slackers. Don't confuse slackers with animosity generators. Slackers avoid *extra* work, not work in general. They are good at what they do, and have social graces. They don't make things harder on others.

Slackers are good to associate with because they have a lot of free time. If you're swamped with your own work, a slacker friend is usually available to do you a solid and help out. It's easy to stay on good terms with a slacker. Whenever the boss asks if you know where the slacker is, just say no.

Transient

Most retail employees fall into the category of transients. Transients are people who decide to work in retail to pay the bills, but do not consider it their career. Transients don't always have an alternate career goal, but the moment an opportunity arises to work outside of retail, they'll usually pounce on it.

Coworkers who don't easily fit into another category can be labeled transients.

Veteran

Anyone who has had long experience in retail who has not become a curmudgeon or attained the enlightenment of a lifer can be considered a veteran. Veterans are career retailers, but not always by choice. Transients automatically flip over into veteran status after ten years of working in retail. Intentional or not, after a decade in the same field, you have to call it a career.

I realize this may be a wake-up call for some of you, but take heart in the fact that you can always *switch* careers.

Weirdo

A weirdo is any employee who routinely makes you feel uneasy. The intensity and nature of a weirdo's weirdness may vary, but there will always be something about him that is unpleasant. A weirdo might stand too close to you when he talks, or stare at you in a piercing way. He may laugh at inappropriate times, or talk to himself a lot.

But there is one bit of unpleasantness that all weirdos seem to have in common—and that's a willingness to talk about their massive porno collections. You can bet that anyone who's glad to chat about the six-foot stack of *Hustler* magazines they have at home isn't exactly a master of propriety. Loose talk about pornography is the true earmark of a weirdo.

Retail weirdos are usually harmless, but you'll probably want to keep your distance anyway. Unless you want to know what kind of smut is legal in Amsterdam . . . weirdo.

Whiner

There's plenty of inequity in retail to complain about, but whiners play the victim card to death. Regardless of the fact that all retail employees go through the same things, a whiner will act as though their own plight is somehow worse than anyone else's. No matter what you've been through, they have it worse. A whiner's favorite phrase is, *"That's nothing, let me tell you what happened to me!"* A whiner always gets the *worst* shifts and the *longest* hours and the *rudest* customers and *boo friggin' hoo!*

The best way to deal with a whiner is to cut them off mid-complaint with some absurd bit of hyperbole. *"Oh yeah? Well, yesterday I was waiting on a customer and he killed me. I'm dead now, can you beat that?"*

CHAPTER 6

The Customers

I f you don't already know, you will quickly learn that much of the stress and headache that come with any retail job is a direct result of dealing with the general public on a daily basis. The myriad of unreasonable and unrealistic expectations floating throughout the mass consciousness of the world all come to rest on the shoulders of salespeople. This is the burden of the retail worker.

This chapter is perhaps the most important one in this book, so it would behoove you to study it thoroughly.

PROBLEM CUSTOMERS

Every customer has the potential to be a problem, but this guide defines "problem customers" as those who exhibit specific annoying behavior as part of their nature.

The following list provides descriptions of the most common problem customers and contains tips on the best ways to deal with them. Keep in mind that many customers will fall into multiple categories, so it's important to be well versed in all of them.

Boomerang Buyer

A boomerang buyer is a habitual consumer who never makes a purchase without first returning a good percentage of the merchandise they purchased on their previous visit. Boomerang buyers are people who are addicted to the cathartic effects of retail therapy, but lack the wherewithal to actually keep the items they purchase. They perpetually recycle the initial investment of some long ago purchase through returns and even exchanges, in order to keep themselves numb from the voids of their desperate, empty lives.

The first time you identify a boomerang buyer you may find yourself feeling pity for them, but you shouldn't. Boomerang buyers are making your job harder to make their own sad lives easier, and the store isn't even making money in the process. They're no different than a crackhead uncle who victimizes his extended family for the sake of his addiction. Boomerang buyers couldn't care less about the time-consuming return/exchange process they constantly put you through, or the merchandise they occasionally damage, just so long as they get their fix.

Once you've identified a boomerang buyer, you need to initiate some tough love by becoming a super salesperson. Whenever the boomerang buyer comes in, make the process of returning items uncomfortable by trying to convince them to reconsider, hounding them with high-pressure add-on selling techniques, and generally trying to get them to spend more money in overt and annoying ways.

Remember, the boomerang buyer is shopping for the enjoyment of it, so if you can remove the joy from their experience, they'll have no choice but to go elsewhere to satisfy their habit. If Uncle Crackhead suddenly finds he's getting less of a high from the junk he buys on the corner, he'll find himself another corner.

Borrower

A borrower is a customer who purchases an item with the intention of using it once, then returning it. Borrowers are generally low-income "players" who like to maintain a façade of personal wealth at the clubs and bars they frequent. By borrowing high-end, fashionable clothing instead of purchasing it, they can maintain the cost-free illusion of financial security by sporting a different trendy outfit every Friday night.

Borrowers tend to shop at stores that have liberal return policies, so they don't have to bother hiding the fact that the items they purchased have been used. Usually they only need to claim that the item in question was uncomfortable in order to get a refund. If you work in one of these stores, there isn't much you can do against a borrower.

However, borrowers do occasionally return items at stores that have strict "unworn" return policies. If you work in one of these establishments, you have to be observant. A borrower will know what you look for when processing a return, so they'll go to great lengths to hide their scam. But if you can find a sign that the item has been used, you can deny the return and the borrower will be finished.

Here's what to look for, so you can bust them and deny their refund:

Scotch Tape

Borrowers will often put tape on the soles of their shoes to prevent them from scuffing while wearing them. Occasionally, they forget to remove the tape before returning them—and it is *sweet* when that happens.

Tape *residue* is usually not enough to deny their return, although it can't hurt to question the borrower about it. At least they'll know you're on to them.

Pet Hair

Borrowers are masters of the lint brush, but if they hooked up with a pet owner that night, they're sunk. There's no way they'll get all that hair off.

Always keep some packing tape handy. When you see pet hair, use a small piece of tape to pat down the garment and show the borrower all the fur they missed.

String

Sometimes, tags just can't be hidden and have to be removed. A common borrower technique is to replace the tags using string or thread. When you see this, point out that it's the twenty-first century and the sweatshop that manufactures your clothing in China lets the children use modern plastic tagging guns nowadays.

Bully

Bullies try to get what they want through intimidation and abuse. Sadly, the technique of demanding special treatment usually works, because any seasoned bully knows that nine times out of ten the customer ends up getting what they want if they put up enough of a stink. I can't tell you how many times I resisted the relentless browbeating of some jerk, only to have the manager or corporate office cave in when he finally went over my head.

There is usually only one good strategy for dealing with a bully—be smug. If you get some bully who thinks he's above the rules, make sure you turn him or her down with a smirk that suggests that you think you're God's gift to Earth. The reason for this is simple. You want to make the bully angry enough to swear—because if the customer swears at you, he automatically forfeits his complaint and has to leave. It's the rule of civilized society.

Between employee and customer, swearing is the one thing that instantly kills an argument. As soon as a curse word is used, the argument is over and the potty mouth loses. It doesn't matter that you yourself swear like a drunken sailor in everyday life; as soon as the customer swears, you get to act offended, claim the moral high ground, and instantly win the argument. Game over.

Demand your refund long enough and you will probably get it. Demand your "fucking refund," and you're banned from the store.

Chatterbox

A chatterbox is a customer who can't ask or answer a question without including insignificant details about their life. A chatterbox can't just ask you where the scented candles are. First they have to tell you a long-winded story about *why* they need scented candles. A chatterbox can't just tell you what size pants they're looking for. First they have to tell you what size they *used* to wear and how much weight they've lost/gained since the last time they went shopping and why.

Unfortunately, there isn't much you can do against a chatterbox. Chatterboxes like to talk, and nothing will dissuade them from doing so. It doesn't matter how obvious you make your disinterest, they'll keep right on yapping.

However, if you are trying to avoid some really heinous task, you can take advantage of a chatterbox and encourage them to elaborate on the already superfluous information they're blabbering about. Helping customers is always a legitimate excuse to put off other work, and an emboldened chatterbox can easily help you kill an hour . . . if you can stomach listening to them that long.

Church Recruiter (CR)

A church recruiter is not really a customer at all, but is actually a member of a fringe religious organization with designs on recruiting you or engaging you in spiritual discussion. Church recruiters usually come in packs of three. One recruiter will do the talking while the other two watch silently. The lead CR will engage you in conversation by pretending to be interested in a product. Then, after sufficiently wasting your time and product knowledge, they will change the subject without so much as a clever segue.

The conversation usually goes like this:

> CR: Hi, I was wondering if you could suggest a good
>   family game.
> EMPLOYEE: Sure. Let's see. Well, Taboo is a good game.
>   You have to get your partner to guess a key word

> without using a group of common words normally
> associated with it. It's a lot of fun.
> CR: Wow, that does sound like fun. You know, at our
> church we like to get back to the basics. Have you
> accepted Jesus as your lord and savior?

Whether you're churchgoing or not, I think most people agree that it's highly inappropriate for someone to buttonhole you under false pretenses at your job, then harass you with a religious agenda. There isn't much sympathy to be had for someone who uses such brazenly rude tactics.

The best way to get even with a church recruiter is to waste *their* time by using their own deceptive tactics back on them. When they go into their routine, pretend to be captivated. Ask questions and seem genuinely interested. Then, when they're good and excited, tell them flatly that you're just messing with them and have no more real interest in joining their church than they had in buying Taboo.

If you're really into dishing out payback, you could actually accept the offer to join the recruiter's church. When you go to their place of worship, sit patiently through the first sermon, and then suddenly whip out a suitcase filled with merchandise and start hawking it to the congregation.

Complainer

Complainers are customers who feel it's their duty to point out and be offended by every minor thing that is wrong with your store, no matter how inconsequential. Here's a true story with a perfect example of a complainer and how to deal with one.

Dr. Spellchecker

In 2000, I was the assistant manager of a small "educational" gift store in a mall. We sold telescopes, world music, fossils, Zen gardens, and a general assortment of pseudo-intellectual garbage.

A man came into the store one day and walked straight over to one of the T-shirts we had displayed on a bust form. The shirt had a glow-in-the-dark human skeleton silk-screened on the front with text indicating the scientific names of each bone. After looking at it for a few moments, he walked up to the counter and asked to speak with the manager.

"The manager isn't here today," I said. "But I'm the assistant manager. Can I help you?"

Agitated, the man said, "Yes, I'm a doctor and I was in here about a month ago. When I was here, I pointed out that your skeleton T-shirt has the name of one of the bones misspelled. The word 'zygomatic' is spelled with a 'Z,' but on the shirt it's misspelled with an 'X.' "

"Really?" I said curiously, not sure where he was going with this.

"Yes, really!" he said sternly. "The man I spoke with at the time said he would report it to your home office, but that obviously hasn't happened because it's still misspelled!" He angrily pointed at the shirt across the store and added in an incredulous tone, "I mean, you're supposed to be an educational store! This is ridiculous! I'm a doctor, you know?"

"Wow," I said in a genuinely sympathetic tone worthy of an Academy Award. "I'm embarrassed that we have that shirt up there. Who did you say you spoke to before?"

A bit calmer now, the man answered, "I don't know. Some guy with a mustache."

"Hmm," I said. "That would be the store manager. Well, I can't be sure whether he informed the main office or not, but I can promise you that I certainly will. Thank you for pointing it out to me."

At this point the man became somewhat deflated. "Yeah, okay. It's just that I'm a doctor and this is supposed to be an educational store . . . they shouldn't make those kinds of mistakes, you know?"

"I agree," I said emphatically and without hesitation. Then I collected all the skeleton T-shirts and put them on the counter behind the register.

With nothing left to argue about, the man left timidly. The

entire exchange lasted less than five minutes and at the end of the day, I put the shirts back out. I never saw the guy again.

Complainers are like political debates on Internet message boards. When there's disagreement, the fight lasts forever, nobody backs down, and nobody ever wins. But when everybody agrees with each other, the topic quickly dies and everybody goes away to a different forum where they can find someone to be at loggerheads with.

When a complainer points out something trivial to you, just agree with their observation. If you won't argue with them, they'll get bored and move on to the next store and try to pick a fight there instead.

Coupon Abuser (CA)

As the name implies, coupon abusers deliberately attempt to circumvent the rules printed on their coupon. A coupon abuser will try to use their coupon on merchandise it doesn't apply to, ask you to ring up items separately to get around the "one per customer" limit, or expect you to supply them with a coupon when they don't have one.

If you don't give a CA what they want, they'll go off on a rant about how unfair it is that they're not allowed to openly cheat the system. They'll argue that the coupon doesn't amount to a good enough discount if it's used correctly. They'll even point out any other cashiers or stores who have let them get away with it in the past, just to serve their own selfish purposes.

"Thanks for hooking me up, now I'm going to rat you out as part of my defense to get the manager to let me do it again."

The only way to deal with a coupon abuser is to just say no. If they want to argue, pawn them off on a manager. In the grand scheme of sucky customers, coupon abusers are par for the course, so you're going to encounter a lot of them. They're minor nuisances, but each one will help to thicken your skin and get you used to being yelled at for no good reason.

Displacer

A displacer is any customer who moves merchandise from its proper location. Most displacers pick up merchandise they intend to buy, then change their mind and leave the item in some random location out of laziness. But many displacers seem to think it's their job to make a mess, picking up items they just want to look at, then carelessly tossing them anywhere.

I used to work part-time at an arts and crafts supply store. Once, while I was straightening up the merchandise in an aisle, a woman stood not three feet away from me systematically pulling little bags of beads off of their pegs. She would look at each one disapprovingly, and then toss them onto a nearby shelf. She just couldn't be bothered to put them back on the peg she just took them off of. Freakin' displacer!

There isn't much you can do against the scourge of displacement. I've tried literally following right behind displacers, instantly picking up after them as they made their mess, hoping to make a point. But they just ignore you, or look at you like you're some kind of freak.

All you can do is take some solace in the fact that displacers are mostly hurting themselves. There isn't much time for customer service when fifty percent of a retail employee's job is consumed by putting stuff back where it goes.

I hope there's a special place in Hell for displacers. I like to think that right now there are thousands of displacers damned to product recovery for all eternity in a store the size of the Grand Canyon.

Dumper

Dumpers are customers who discard trash among the shelves and merchandise, sometimes causing product damage in the process. Dumpers are the epitome of laziness. Despite the fact that every store and mall has a multitude of convenient trash receptacles, dumpers just can't be bothered to carry that half-eaten muffin or unfinished coffee back out with them. Instead, they'll just toss it inside a rack of clothing, or tuck it behind a box.

In my fifteen-plus years in retail, I never once caught a dumper in the act of dumping, so I have no practical advice on how to deal with them. Although I always promised myself that if I ever *did* catch a dumper, I would pick up their trash and discreetly follow them out to the parking lot. Then as they drove off, I would hum the trash at their rear windshield and book it.

I always imagined the garbage to be something that would explode dramatically on impact—like a large Orange Julius, or a soft drink loaded with crushed ice.

Fisher

A fisher is a customer who melodramatically pantomimes frustration, or loudly asks a question to someone they're with in the hopes that a salesperson will catch on and ask them if they need help. Fishers believe that salespeople should be perceptive enough to realize when they need help without them having to say anything, so they can't bring themselves to ask for help directly.

What fishers fail to realize is that all retail employees have collectively learned through experience that the vast majority of customers actually become irritated when you ask them if they want help. Most consumers don't know the difference between "attentive" and "pushy," so it's not worth the trouble. The most hassle-free tactic for a retail employee is to greet each customer, then leave him or her alone. If they need help, all they have to do is ask.

Another thing fishers don't seem to realize is how annoying their passive/aggressive behavior is. Heavy sighs, furrowed brows, and flapping arms are things that children do to get attention. When my daughter acts like that, I tell her to "use your words." Saying that to a customer who's acting the same way would be extremely funny, but I can't recommend doing that in good conscience.

Even more annoying is a fisher who tries to get your attention by loudly asking their child the question they need answered. It's amazing that anyone can be ignorant of how silly they look when they ask their eight-month-old, *"Gosh, Jacob, I wonder if they have any more AAA batteries. I don't see any more out here, do you? Do you think they have any more out back?"*

It's your call how you want to handle a fisher. You can either ignore them until they break down and ask for help like a big boy or girl, or you can just give in and ask them what they need. As much as you may hate to send the wrong message, it's usually a lot easier to let the fisher win. Some fishers will huff and puff to themselves or talk through their kids for a long time before breaking down, so it's often worth it to just deal with them quickly.

Flawyer

A flawyer is a customer who uses their uneducated misinterpretation of the law in an attempt to make a point or get what they want. Flawyers like to accuse you of "false advertising" or "bait and switch," without the faintest grasp of what those legal concepts actually mean. Flawyers also mistakenly believe that possession of a receipt is an absolute legal guarantee that they can return an item for a full cash refund at any time and that the terms "all sales final," "within sixty days," and "unopened" carry no actual weight.

You can easily shut a flawyer up by showing them that you understand the concept they're accusing you of better than they do. In a nutshell, here is the definition of the two legal principles that are most commonly misunderstood by flawyers.

False Advertising

False advertising is the misrepresentation of a price, product, or service. If I run an ad that says my shoes are handmade by skilled craftsmen in Italy, but my shoes are really made on machines by children in Pakistan, I am guilty of false advertising.

If, on the other hand, I run an ad that says I have toothbrushes on sale, but I sell out of those toothbrushes before everyone in the state has a chance to come buy one, I am only guilty of poor planning or low expectations.

Bait and Switch

When a retailer advertises a product or service that it has no real intention of selling, for the sole purpose of attracting customers and steering them to a more expensive product or service, it's called a "bait and switch." The victim will often find the advertised item is unavailable or has hidden conditions that make it undesirable.

On the other hand, when a retailer advertises an item on sale, but the salespeople try to get you to buy a more expensive item instead, it's called "trying to get a bigger commission." The victim can still purchase the sale item if they want to and should stop being such a whiny baby.

Haggler

Hagglers always attempt to bargain for a discount, even when it should be obvious that the staff has no authority to modify the marked prices. It boggles the mind how far removed some people can be from the way things really work. How anyone could think that the floor help at Home Depot has the power to arbitrarily knock ten or twenty bucks off a jigsaw is beyond me. Haggling is to be expected at car dealerships or rummage sales, but not at the grocery store.

Most hagglers are fairly harmless. As soon as you tell them in no uncertain terms that you have no control over the prices, they'll usually leave you alone. However, some hagglers will have the audacity to ask you if you'll hook them up with your employee discount. Whenever that happened to me, I would always tell the customer that I would, but only if he or she went in the back and ran stock for the next six hours.

Feel free to be ruder than that. When a haggler crosses the line and asks you to commit fraud on their behalf, all bets are off. You can treat them however you want.

Kook

A kook is a customer who exhibits odd behavior or doesn't seem to be playing with a full deck. There is no real defense against a kook. Once you get stuck with some random crazy person who wanders into your store, you've got to deal with him or her until they leave. One of the most important skills you can learn in retail is how to spot a kook before you get stuck listening to some government conspiracy theory or diatribe on the end times.

Here are some red flags to look out for:

- Wild hair/eyes
- Too much makeup
- Crazy hat
- Talking to themselves
- Singing (without iPod)
- Laughing for no discernible reason
- Creepy eight-inch fingernails

Lingerer

A lingerer is a customer who dawdles in the store long after the closing announcement has been made and the doors have been locked. Lingerers have no respect or common courtesy. In their mind, it's perfectly acceptable to wander into a store five minutes before closing and then browse for half an hour.

No matter how many times you ask if they need help or announce that the store is closed over the loudspeaker, lingerers won't take the hint. When they finally make it up to the front of the store, they'll act shocked when they see the entire staff sitting pissed-off at the registers and say, *"Oh, are you closed? I'm sorry, I had no idea."*

Unfortunately, many stores make it a policy never to rush a

customer or ask them to leave, so the only way to deal with a lingerer is to make them uncomfortable. Rudeness deserves rudeness. After the second announcement is ignored, a more personal message should be repeated every two minutes to get the point across. Such as, *"Good evening, lady in the red coat. Just so you know, we closed ten minutes ago"* or, *"Attention, man in the blue shorts. Are you done yet? Just curious."*

If you don't have an intercom, you can follow the lingerer around the store and stare at them with your arms crossed, or whistle a tune over and over again. If you need to, you can up the pressure by saying things like, *"Are you sure I can't help you with anything?"* or, *"You know we're closed, right? Just checking."*

Neanderthal

A Neanderthal is any customer who is socially inept on even the most basic level. Neanderthals lack the ability to return greetings, or say "thank you" or "excuse me." Most won't speak at all unless it's absolutely necessary. Even then, they will only communicate in angry monosyllabic grunts. Neanderthals are easily frustrated, so if they can't find what they want, they'll just storm out instead of asking questions.

"Thog no ask question! Question for weak! Thog strong! No have jean in Thog size! Thog no like to use fitting room! Thog take business elsewhere!"

The most annoying Neanderthal trait is their inability to

handle cash with any grace. They'll just smash their money on the counter, or rip bills out of your hand.

"Thog take change like warrior!"

Neanderthals are annoying, but basically innocuous. Just do your best to ignore their behavior. They don't want you to talk to them or help them and they're not capable of focusing their anger into a letter to corporate, so you never have to worry about pleasing them.

"Thog not happy with selection! Thog go home! Thog throw things and yell at cat! Thog feel better."

Nitpicker

Nitpickers are customers who will look for an insignificant flaw in a garment or product and point it out in order to get a discount. Nitpickers will grouse over the tiniest stitch out of place or a nearly invisible scratch and act as if you were trying to sell them leftovers from the Salvation Army. Of course, the nitpicker is always willing to *own* the merchandise that they claim is so obviously flawed and substandard—so long as they can get a better price. In a nitpicker's mind, nothing is too imperfect to buy, but everything is imperfect enough to be discounted.

The best way to handle a nitpicker is to use their logic against them. When they allege that a shirt has one sleeve that is several microns shorter than the other, agree with their assertion that such shoddy merchandise can't be sold at full price. Then insist that it be removed from the sales floor at once, for fear that selling it at all might soil your store's good reputation. Thank the nitpicker for their keen observation and tell them that you will call the vendor immediately and demand a refund.

If the nitpicker still doesn't give up, excuse yourself and march to a nearby floor phone to have an imaginary argument with the manufacturer. If you happen to speak Laotian, Hindi, or any other Eastern language, use it to add realism to your pretend phone call.

Pack Rat

Pack rats fill their shopping carts with items that they don't necessarily intend to purchase. A typical pack rat will wait until they get to the counter before they decide which of their items they want to keep, with total disregard for the line that inevitably forms behind them. The pack rat will then leisurely contemplate each of the many items in their carriage and unload all the unwanted merchandise on you.

More efficient pack rats will make their decision before they get to the register, and hand you their voted down items right away, or ditch them among the impulse merchandise displayed near the counter.

Most retailers will supply each register with a plastic bin to accommodate the steady stream of pack rats the cashiers will get throughout the day. Ideally, the merchandise in these bins would be periodically returned to its proper location, but realistically it just gets dumped into larger bins behind the customer service desk until the end of the night. Then all the employees spend hours whittling away at the giant pile of random merchandise after the store closes.

Curiously, pack rats seem to think their methods are normal. Often a pack rat will start unloading items onto the counter without a word, then act genuinely surprised when you start ringing them up. Astonished, they'll say, "Whoa! I'm not buying that!" As if it were presumptuous of you to think they planned on purchasing all the items they took off the shelf, put in their cart, brought to the register, and placed on the counter.

Like displacers, there's nothing you can do to dissuade pack rats. Just try to appreciate the instant karma those same customers get stuck with when they can't get any help on the sales floor because the entire staff is constantly busy reshelving merchandise.

Peripheral Hoverer (PH)

A peripheral hoverer is a customer who hangs just within the limits of your vision and stares at you until you ask if they need help. A close relative of the fisher, the peripheral hoverer also believes that you should be perceptive enough to know when they need help, even when you are clearly focused on some task. Instead of sighing or talking through their kids to get your attention, they stare at you like some psychopath until you can literally feel their presence and need for assistance.

Peripheral hoverers are slightly less annoying than fishers, but they still deserve to incur a penalty for their childish behavior. The next time you feel the piercing stare of a PH trying to say "excuse me" with their mind, count to sixty in your head before acknowledging them. Be sure to count slowly, too. Use the "Mississippi" method, so it takes a full minute.

Theoretically, if this annoying social aberration is punished consistently, peripheral hoverers will eventually become extinct as a matter of evolutionary convenience. Although I expect to be driving a mass-produced, zero-emission, hydrogen-fuel-cell vehicle before that happens.

Philosophers

Philosophers are customers who try to bestow some hackneyed wisdom upon you when they catch you in a bad mood. If I had a nickel for every customer who dished out the secret of life in the form of some oversimplified philosophy, I'd have about $30—which isn't a lot of money, but that's 600 nickels!

Nobody likes to have their feelings summarily invalidated by complete strangers, and that's exactly what philosophers do. There are two different types of philosophers who have distinct ideologies that they will try to impart when they catch you being human on the sales floor.

Philosopher Type A

"If you don't like your job, you should get a different one."

Well that's brilliant advice. I'm sure the dean will let you skip the next four years of college and give you your degree on good faith, so you can start working at the law firm tomorrow.

It never occurs to the type A philosopher that you might actually have a plan for ascending above your current crappy job sometime in the future, or that you might be looking for a better job already. No, they're so self-righteous that they just can't let you be angry about whatever job-related injustice you've recently suffered. Type A philosophers like their jobs, so they figure everyone else should too—it's that simple.

The fact of the matter is there aren't enough dream jobs to go around. The vast majority of the world has to work doing something they don't enjoy to pay the bills. Most people learn to accept the crap their job dishes out on a regular basis, but no one should be expected to eat it with a smile.

You can quickly teach this kind of philosopher to mind his own business by confessing that it's really some made-up personal problem that's making you irritable—the more uncomfortable the better.

"Sigh. It's not really the job that's getting me down. I got my girlfriend's mom pregnant and I just don't know how to break it to her. What do you think I should do?"

Not only will it send them packing, but the discomfort you cause them will make you feel better and get your mind off what made you angry in the first place.

Philosopher Type B
"Smile!"

Nothing makes a bad mood worse than a type B philosopher who gets in your face with an oh-so-punchable grin and says, "Smile, you'll feel better!"

Type B philosophers want you to join them in the emotionally numb cocoon of delusional happiness they live in, but don't be fooled into thinking they have your well-being in mind—they're only catering to their own ego. Type B philosophers see it as a feather in their cap when they get someone to drink the Kool-Aid with them. They're only doing it to feel better about themselves. Besides, only lunatics smile when they're angry.

The easiest way to send a type B philosopher on their way is to offer your best grimace and say, "I *am* smiling." This usually gets the point across, but if you run into an especially persistent philosopher there's a chance that it will only encourage them to tell you, "It takes more muscles to frown than it does to smile!" or some similar BS. If that happens, just use the girlfriend's mother story again. That should do the trick.

Prodder

A prodder is a customer who touches you physically when they want your assistance. Whether it's an elbow nudge to the upper arm or a finger jab to the shoulder blade, prodders seem to believe that it's acceptable to use the same technique to get your attention as one would use to start a bar fight.

Fortunately, prodders are relatively rare, so you shouldn't have to deal with them too often. When you do get one, it's best to just let their behavior slide. Anyone who goes around jabbing complete strangers has probably seen his or her share of fights (fights that were most likely started when they poked the wrong person), so unless you know karate or something, you should just walk away.

Reeker

Be it from BO, halitosis, or just plain filth, a reeker is any customer who smells badly because of poor hygiene. We've all had days when we needed to run an errand in less than "shower fresh" condition, but there is a difference between the BO of someone who has been working hard all day and the reek of someone who's spent the last week sitting on a couch eating Twizzlers and Cool Ranch Doritos. Everyone has bad breath from time to time, but there's a definite disparity between the pungent exhalation of someone who just ate a sandwich loaded with onions and the fetor of a mouth that has never been introduced to floss.

There just isn't any good excuse for reeking in public. If someone can smell you from a distance of more than three feet, you've got a serious problem. Even if one were to give a reeker the benefit of the doubt and assume that instead of poor hygiene, they simply fell into a septic tank on their way to JCPenney, they still should have gone home first to clean up.

Like kooks, the best defense against a reeker is to learn how to spot them early so you can avoid them before you end up inside their stink radius.

Here are some red flags to look out for:

- Greasy hair peppered with pillow lint
- Several missing front teeth
- Stained clothes (particularly the crotch and pit areas)
- Crumbs on shirt
- Dirty graphic T-shirt from an outdated TV show *not* meant ironically (e.g., *Alf, Mr. Belvedere, BJ and the Bear*)
- Other shoppers/employees being visibly repulsed

Slosher

A slosher is a customer who is intoxicated. Sloshers are most commonly encountered during night shifts, but it is not at all out of the ordinary to run into one during the day. It has never ceased to amaze me how many people are lit at 11 o'clock in the morning.

How you deal with a slosher depends on what kind of slosher you run into. There are two types of sloshers—"happy" and "angry."

Happy Sloshers: lovable drunks of the Foster Brooks variety. They stumble around a bit and ramble incoherently, but they rarely cause any problems and are almost always amusing. They help to break up the day and provide you with an interesting story to tell.

Happy sloshers are easy to handle.

Angry Sloshers: people who become belligerent or crazy when they're drunk. They'll swear at you for no reason, accuse you of insane things, or act in an overall irate way for no obvious reason.

Alcohol Abused

I once had a job working at a convenience store. One night a slosher stumbled in from the bar next door to buy cigarettes. As he asked for his brand he stared at me with a strangely dubious expression on his face. I just figured it was because he was drunk, so I gave him his smokes and took his money, but after the transaction was completed he just stood there and kept staring at me.

"Do you need anything else?" I said, wondering if he was maybe looking behind me at the rolling papers or the *Playboys*.

His expression turned to one of dim recognition and he said in an angry yet strangely nonchalant tone, "You're the fucking guy who burned my house up."

"What?" I said, bemused both by the absurd accusation and the notion of burning one's house "up" as opposed to "down."

A sly smile came to his face and he said, "Don't act like you don't pretend to know. I know. I'll be back for you burning up my house. Don't think you'll forget, because you won't." Again, his tone of voice was angry, but remarkably calm for someone who apparently thought he had just run into the man responsible for burning up his house.

"Um, I have no idea what you're talking about," I returned matter-of-factly.

He stood staring for what seemed like a long time, before finally asking, "Can I get some matches?"

I furrowed my brow, confused, but obliged him by tossing a pack of matches onto the counter.

He packed his cigarettes on the heel of his hand, unwrapped them, picked out the foil and tossed it on the counter for me to throw away. He lit up a smoke, shook out the match and tossed it on the floor. He took a drag, exhaled in my general direction, then said, "I think it's yours."

I couldn't think of anything constructive to say to that, so I just looked at him blankly and hoped I wouldn't have to call the cops.

Luckily, after a few more seconds of staring, he took one more drag, then left.

When it comes to an angry slosher, the less you say the better. Since the drink in them is fueling their demented thought process, it's useless to attempt reasoning with them. Just remain calm and try not to say anything confrontational, and they'll usually forget what they were talking about and leave.

Of course, the behavior of some angry sloshers is beyond patiently waiting for them to go. When a slosher rips his shirt off and starts kicking over displays, it's time to involve the authorities. You don't get paid anywhere near enough to deal with that kind of crap.

Sobby

A sobby is a customer who attempts to gain your sympathy with some hard luck story. Sobbies typically try to get you to give them a discount from an expired sale, or let them into the store five minutes after closing. They'll tell you some sad tale about how their car broke down the day of the sale, or how it's someone's birthday tomorrow and they need a gift, so you just *have* to let them in or the party will be ruined! A sobby will beg and plead on the verge of tears, desperately appealing to you to grant them a single ray of sunshine in the otherwise melodramatic tragedy of their life.

All I can say is don't be suckered in. If you wait until 9:25 p.m. the night before your kid's birthday to go out and buy a present, then you're a procrastinator beyond reproach and I have no sympathy for you. If you missed the sale, tough—wait for the next one. Anyone who expects you to believe they couldn't find a way to get to your store during any of the eighty-six hours it was open last week to hit a sale or get what they needed is either a liar or lazy beyond imagination.

Door Duty

I once worked part-time in an arts-and-crafts supply store. One night at closing, I was on "door duty," which means standing at the store entrance to prevent other customers from coming in while you wait for all the lingerers to leave.

A woman approached and I told her, "Sorry, we're closed."

"I thought you were open until 10:00?" she said despondently. Genuinely sympathetic, I said, "No, we close at 9:30."

"But, I only need one thing," she rebutted, using a standard customer rationale. "I'll be really quick. I know exactly what I want."

"Sorry, you'll have to come back tomorrow," I said coldly. I always dropped the sympathy whenever customers begged or got needy.

She looked at me as if I had just denied her access to some life-saving medical procedure, then broke into the most pathetic excuse I've ever heard. "Can you please let me in? I work all day and I can never get here before your store closes."

I just looked at her, honestly dumbfounded. It was the most

implausible thing I'd ever heard. The store was open thirteen hours a day Monday through Saturday and seven hours on Sunday, yet she could *never* get to our store while it was open? Where the hell did she work? Was she commuting through time to a nineteenth-century London workhouse, where they forced her to work fourteen hours a day? Even then, she would get Sunday off. Her assertion was completely ridiculous.

"Sorry," I repeated simply.

Immediately, her Sally Sad face turned into a visage of hate not completely unlike Emperor Palpatine from *Star Wars*. "Thanks for nothing!" she shouted angrily and stormed off.

Space Invader

A space invader is a customer who has no concept of personal space. Despite the fact that you are visibly recoiling and backpedaling, space invaders don't see anything wrong with leaning in like they're about to give you a kiss just to ask you what aisle the glue is in. I honestly don't know how anyone could make it to adulthood without learning the conventions of personal boundaries. You'd think that it would be impossible to make it past twenty years of age before getting beaten for flagrantly sliding in to share the wrong person's breathing space.

Over the years, I've developed a defense against space invaders called the "grab and block." Because space invaders can look like anyone, you're not likely to see them coming, so you need to learn how to initiate the G&B quickly.

The Grab and Block Technique

Step 1.

Step 2.

Step 3.

1. When you see a space invader descending upon you, immediately break eye contact, turn away, and take three quick paces backward, acting as if you don't realize they are about to ask you a question. You only have seconds before the space invader corrects his trajectory and gets back in front of you, so you have to move to step 2 quickly.
2. Grab a piece of nearby merchandise. A medium or large item works best, but you can make do with a small item if necessary.
3. Hold the merchandise at arm's length, pretending to examine it for some reason.

You have now set up an effective block and can acknowledge the space invader from a comfortable distance. Maintain the shield until the space invader is gone. If the odd and unnecessary way you are continuing to hold the merchandise is questioned, just brush it off with a vague, "no reason" or "just because." Space invaders by nature aren't very socially adroit, so they're not likely to question you beyond that.

Important: Space invaders who are also reekers pose a serious threat. The G&B technique could save your life!

Tagger

Taggers are customers who read your nametag, then use your name in every single sentence for the duration of their visit. Taggers are under the delusion that using your name over and over again is going to appeal to your ego on some level, encourage you to be more attentive to their needs, and provide them with better service.

The problem with this tagger theory is that using a total

stranger's first name over and over again with the motive of gaining their favor is going to be interpreted as either weird or insultingly transparent. Taggers almost always provoke the exact opposite response they intended.

A salesperson who's unaware of the common ways business people have been manipulating their peers since the 1950s is going to think the tagger who unnecessarily keeps repeating their name is some kind of wacko. A salesperson who's more sociologically perceptive is going to be instantly turned off by such an obvious con. Either way, it's annoying and the salesperson is going to try ditching the tagger ASAP.

The best way to deal with a tagger is to give them a taste of their own medicine. After they've started using your name excessively, ask them what their name is. When they tell you, start using their handle in every sentence.

"Well Derek, we have two different types of tool sets. We have the 64-piece set with metric socket wrench, Derek. But I highly recommend the deluxe 128-piece set, Derek. It's more expensive, Derek, but it's a better, Derek, value, Derek."

Either they'll pretend it doesn't bother them or they'll get mad and walk away, but it will get the point across. You don't have to worry about getting in trouble, because they can't fault you for doing what they're doing without coming clean about trying to manipulate you in the first place.

It's not like they can say, *"Hey, I was trying to butter up your associate by using his name a lot, so then he got smart and started using my name excessively!"*

Threatener

FIELD GUIDE TO CUSTOMERS

The Threatener
(Insubstantialis Ultimatum)

Threateners make idle threats to get what they want or to make a point. The two most common empty threats are *"I'm writing a letter to your home office!"* and *"I'm never shopping here again."*

Threateners are easy to deal with because they rarely carry through with their threats. The type of person who would actually write a nasty letter to corporate to get you in trouble would never give you any fair warning beforehand—they want to bombshell you with it so you don't have the opportunity to come up with a good defense for whatever it is you supposedly did. Anyone who *threatens* you with a missive to corporate is just trying to scare you up front because they're too lazy to do the work of writing a real letter.

The type of person who threatens to never again visit your store has done nothing but put you in a win/win situation. If they do come back in again, you get the satisfaction of calling them on their bluff. If they don't come back again . . . well, they don't come back again. Where's the downside?

Whistler

A whistler is a customer who makes loud noises to get your attention. A less offensive cousin of the prodder, a whistler whoops, hollers, whistles, or shouts for your service rather than inconvenience themselves by traversing a distance of twenty feet.

Whistlers have somehow remained blissfully unaware that the protocols surrounding retail and service industry workers have changed since 1933. A loud finger whistle is useful for hailing a cab or calling your dog in the modern world, but that's about it.

Whistlers generally expect the same service standards they would expect from a depression-era bellhop, so it's best to avoid them if you can. The trick is training yourself to ignore loud whistles. The instinctual reaction to turn toward loud noises is hard to overcome, but with practice you can learn to block out specific sounds—like the "hey you" whistle or crying babies.

If you can stop yourself from looking in the direction of a whistle or shout for "service!" you can immediately try to vanish among the aisles, but still claim ignorance if they catch up with you. In the absence of eye contact you always have plausible deniability.

Note: If you work in a small store, you won't be able to avoid whistlers, but you can always play dumb and stare at them with a confused expression when they call for you, as if you had no idea what they were trying to tell you. It makes the whistler suffer a minor nuisance and could possibly discourage them from wasting their time with the outdated technique in the future.

UNREALISTIC EXPECTATIONS

It isn't only problem customers who cause grief. Regular customers can give you a headache, too. Much of the aggravation that surrounds working with customers stems from the fact that the general public has a lot of misconceptions and unrealistic expectations when it comes to retail.

When confronted with the unrealistic expectations of a customer, many retail employees make the mistake of pointing out the error in their logic or attempting to educate them on how things really work. This is a complete waste of time. By nature, people with unrealistic expectations can't handle the truth, so it's much easier and far more efficient to lie to them.

You can avoid a lot of annoyance on the sales floor by learning how to deal with unrealistic expectations. Here are a few examples of how customers think and what you can do to get rid of them.

Why don't you sell the ridiculously esoteric item I want?

Some customers believe that their personal needs automatically translate into a product demand, so they become upset when a store is mysteriously lacking in the supply. They figure if they need a pair of spats and an ivory-handled riding crop, then the rest of the world must need them, too.

Sometimes these customers will become agitated when they find you're not stocked to the hilt with copper-plated spittoons or six-inch replicas of the Arc de Triomphe. When this happens, your instinct might be to defend your store's choice not to sell the item, but don't bother. The customer will only become angrier and obstinately dispute your reasoning no matter how obvious it is.

Your best course of action is to invent a store that does carry the item in question. Give the store a realistic-sounding name, place it in the mall in the next town over and send them on their way. The false hope will stop them from taking their frustration out on you and quickly get them out the door. Just remember to speak about the fictitious store in uncertain terms in case you happen to run into the same customer again.

"The last time I was at the Smithfield Mall, they had a little store called the Spittoon Emporium down one of the side corridors. I don't remember which one, but I'll bet they have what you're looking for."

This may sound like a jerky thing to do, but so is giving attitude to the floor help in some random store because you can't
find what you want.

*Note: Whatever you do, don't send the customer on a wild goose chase to a
real store. You wouldn't want one of your retail brothers or sisters doing
that to you.*

You should give out coupons in the store!

Every few weeks or so, your store may put ads or flyers in the local newspaper. Sometimes, those flyers have coupons in them.
The result is a mutually beneficial symbiosis. People will buy
the newspaper just to get your store's coupon and people who
already buy the newspaper will see your store's ad. Everybody
wins.

Some customers, however, don't see why they should take
part in this relationship. They just want the discount. They figure that if there's a coupon in existence, they should be given
one without having to search for it or cut it out of the paper.

The unrealistic expectation here is that retailers should shell
out a ton of money on newspaper ads to drive business by giving out discounts, but not care if the whole process is undermined by lazy customers who don't think they should have to
spend fifty cents to get a 40-percent off coupon. I'm not one to
whip out the world's tiniest violin for big corporate retail
chains, but on principle I side with them on this one. They're
offering a discount to anyone who cuts a little square out of the
newspaper—if a customer can't be bothered to do that much,
then screw them—they don't deserve it.

Of course you'll never pull at anyone's heartstrings with that
garbage, so you have to take a different approach. When a customer gives you flak about not giving out extra coupons, just
play the big brother card. Tell them you'd really like to give
them an extra coupon, but you can't—the evil corporate office
painstakingly counts every coupon and you'll get fired if you're
short even one.

Pretending that you'd help them out if your hands weren't tied will usually get them to drop the subject and turn their anger toward corporate . . . which admittedly doesn't deserve it in this instance, but hey . . . it's corporate, so who cares?

Besides, the bit about them counting coupons is usually true.

Can I use your bathroom?

If your store doesn't have public restrooms, you're going to get this question a lot. Some people seem to expect others to give the benefit of the doubt to them in situations where they would never do the same. If a total stranger knocked on your door at home and asked to use your bathroom because they just couldn't hold it anymore, would you let them? The fact that it's a store doesn't change the principle. Retailers don't have the manpower to keep an eye on every slouch off the street who needs to use the can. Nobody should expect unsupervised access to the back room of a store.

Understandably, retailers don't want the liability of customers wandering willy-nilly through the stockroom, so they almost always make it a policy to deny customers access to their non-public restrooms. Despite your telling the customer that, they're likely to try convincing you to let them use the toilet anyway. They'll beg and plead and tell you how badly they or their kids have to go, insisting that they could never make it to the nearby mall restrooms or the department store across the parking lot without soiling themselves.

Before you feel sorry for the next person who comes along with their legs pinched together, allow me to share a story with you.

No Good Deed Goes Unpunished

This incident took place at the men's shoe store I used to manage. It was a little boutique-type store in a mall. We had a small, cramped stockroom with a single tiny bathroom, just big enough to fit a toilet and little pedestal sink.

I was working alone one slow afternoon, when two older women entered the store. One woman was in her early forties and the other was in her mid-sixties, presumably her mother.

The younger woman said, "Excuse me, can we use your bathroom? It's a bit of an emergency."

The store was at an unfortunate central point in the mall that was about as far as you could be from any public restroom, so I was used to getting the question. "I'm sorry, it's against our company policy," I said automatically. "There's a public restroom in Sears, though. If you get on the escalator . . ."

The younger woman cut me off desperately, "I know, but she's not going to make it. She has a weak bladder. Please, we'll only be a minute!"

I should point out that the older woman whom she was with and referring to did not seem infirm or in any degree of discomfort, but I was taken in by the embarrassing disclosure. If it was a lie, it was a good one.

"All right," I sighed. "It's right in the back, you can't miss it."

"Oh, thank you," she said, and the two of them went into the back room together.

Just as they went back, a customer came in to pick up some shoes he had ordered. He wanted to try them on before leaving, so I took him to a chair and started lacing up the shoes for him.

No sooner did I get the shoes on his feet than a loud "Oh, no!" came from the back room. Displeased by this portent of things to come, I excused myself from my customer and rushed to the stockroom.

Both women were standing outside the bathroom dancing to avoid the pool of toilet water that was quickly oozing out onto the stockroom floor.

"The toilet overflowed!" said the younger woman, distressed.

Stifling my urge to swear loudly and repeatedly, I quickly splashed through the fresh sewage into the bathroom. The tank was still filling, so I bent down to turn the shutoff valve behind the toilet, accidentally dipping my tie into the bowl in the process.

"I didn't even use very much toilet paper," said the older woman defensively. "I think there's something wrong with the toilet."

Rather than beating them both with the toilet brush, I was somehow able to ignore the comment and use it to fish out the beehive-size wad of tissue clogging the bowl instead. As the water drained, I removed my wet tie and threw it in the sink.

"Hello?" called my customer from the sales floor. I had forgotten about him.

I went out to the counter where the customer was waiting with his shoes. "These are fine. Can I just get a bag?"

"Sure," I said apologetically. "Sorry about that."

He looked at me oddly as I bagged his shoes, no doubt noticing that my tie was mysteriously gone. "No problem."

After he left, I returned to find the younger woman had unraveled an entire roll of paper towels onto the flood in a weak attempt to clean it up. Now, instead of simply mopping it up, I had to pick up a huge bundle of soaking wet paper first. Furthermore, we had no rubber gloves, so I had to use my bare hands.

As much as I would have preferred that they simply leave at that point, the women insisted on milling about guiltily while I cleaned up the mess. After I got the paper towels picked up, I began mopping. Luckily, the decades of dust and crud beneath the shelving had acted as a barrier and kept the water from seeping underneath.

When I finally had it cleaned up, the women said they were sorry. At this point in my career I was already a retail veteran, so my default servitude setting kicked in and accepted the apology. "Don't worry about it," I said resignedly. "It's no big deal."

Then, on the way out, the older woman tried to lighten the mood and said, "At least you don't have to wash the floor now."

I gave her a weak smile and nod, thinking to myself, "*Yeah, I always mop the floor with pissy shit-water from the toilet.*"

When my assistant came in later, I had to buy a new mop and spend another hour cleaning the floor.

The most effective lie to use when a customer wants to use your bathroom is to tell them it's out of order. They probably won't believe you, but they're in no real position to argue.

Note: It helps if every employee is on the same page with the bathroom lie. That way the customer can't trip you up by unexpectedly asking a second employee the same thing.

I broke this, so I'd like a refund

Perhaps the most unreasonable expectation is the presumption that a retailer should replace an item that the customer accidentally (or intentionally) destroys. I've squared off with countless customers who bring some broken toy or electronic gadget up to the counter with a disgusted look on their face, suggesting that it's the quality of the merchandise that's at fault. Some customers seem to think that "defective" and "unable to withstand a four-foot vertical drop" mean the same thing.

If you work in a store that has one of those insane "unconditional return" policies, then there isn't much you can do when this happens. Personally, I think those stores deserve whatever they get. They might as well hang a sign on the door that says "Abuse Us!"

If you have a normal return policy, then you'll have to decline the ridiculous assertion that you should take responsibility for the customer's negligence. There's no good lie that will quickly get rid of a customer who's mad because you won't take back their broken stuff. But instead of reiterating the store's return policy over and over again, you can quickly dispatch the customer using a "car analogy." The car analogy theory goes like this:

Store policy regarding any merchandise instantly becomes clear and irrefutable when an analogy is made using a theoretical automobile purchase.

The car analogy works every time. There's nothing you can argue the point with. Once you make a car analogy, the argument is over. You win.

- If you bought a car and backed it into a telephone pole, you wouldn't expect the dealership to take it back, would you?

- If you refused to purchase a warranty on a car, you wouldn't expect the dealership to repair it for free if it broke down, would you?
- If you bought a car, you wouldn't expect the dealership to replace your tires or windshield wipers for free, would you?
- If you never changed the oil in your car, you wouldn't expect it to run well, would you?

There's something about comparing merchandise to a car that crystallizes any point. Use car analogies frequently.

Ironically, there is no effective analogy that can be used when the merchandise in question actually is an automobile. Sorry, car dealers, I've got nothing for you.

I know you're closed, but I still want to come in

It isn't just sobbies who will try to get into your store after closing; a lot of regular customers expect you to play loosey-goosey with the store hours, too. Rather than hit you with a sob story, they'll look at you with disdain and bust out some cracked logic, saying something like, "I only need one thing!" or "My watch says it's 9:28!"—as if you're just a lazy cretin who wants to go home as early as possible.

Of course the unrealistic expectation here is that an entire store full of employees should make a personal sacrifice at no benefit to themselves so that one person can shop whenever they please. Besides, if you've ever made the mistake of letting someone in after closing, you know that customer is going to instantly forget everything they promised you at the door. The "one item" they swore would only take them "two seconds" to get will invariably turn into four items twenty minutes later.

Rather than argue with some self-serving logic at the door, the fastest way to shut them up and send them home is by creating a physical impossibility to an after-hours purchase. Just tell the customer that the registers are already closed and the computer system won't allow you to reopen them until morning. They probably won't believe you and they'll definitely go away mad, but at least they'll go away.

These types of customers always remind me of that episode of *The Brady Bunch* where they had a contest building a house of cards to decide whether the boys or the girls would get to choose what their combined trading stamps got spent on. In the end, the girls won and they all rushed to the redemption center, but it was already closed. They banged on the door and turned into a bunch of sobbies until the curmudgeonly clerk finally let them in. They promised to be quick, but once they got in they couldn't decide whether they wanted the sewing machine or the canoe, so the clerk was screwed.

I always felt bad for that poor guy. Especially since the plot involved this particular trading-stamp company going out of business. The poor sap was about to be unemployed and half of the heartless Brady bunch just sobby-suckered him into working late.

Frickin' Bradys.

I'm used to getting what I want!

Some customers have a sense of entitlement that defies all logic. Whether the attitude comes from being powerful or privileged in their everyday life, or just a spoiled upbringing, some people think they have the world coming to them.

The only advice I can give you concerning the reality challenged is to stick to your guns. Don't ever bend the rules or give preferential treatment to anyone simply because they think they're better than everyone else.

Here's an example of one of the most egregious cases of self-entitlement I've seen and how it was handled in the exact wrong way.

It's Your Fault I'm an Idiot

I was once the assistant manager of a shoe store located on a narrow but busy street in a major metropolitan area.

One day the district manager was doing a store visit. He was talking to the store manager and me at the counter when a man came in to return a pair of shoes.

He plopped the bag on the counter. "I need to return these."

Being the lowest man present on the manager totem pole, I knew it was my duty to bow out of the conversation and handle it, so I took the shoebox out of the bag and opened it up. Inside was a pair of cordovan wingtips that had been worn a few times. There were no obvious defects, so I asked, "Was there anything wrong with them?"

"They're uncomfortable," he replied tersely.

We had a thirty-day unconditional guarantee on our shoes, so he was well within his right to return them, but we were trained to try to cut our losses when customers took us up on it. "Oh, well that's okay. Would you like to try something else on? Maybe exchange them for something different?"

"No, I don't have time today," he said simply.

"Okay," I said acceptingly. I rang up the return and refunded the man's money. "Sorry they didn't work out for you."

As the man left, the manager gave me the "oh, well" look and I rejoined him and the DM in conversation.

Less than a minute later, the man stormed back in waving a parking ticket over his head. "I just got ticketed in front of your store!" he yelled.

Before I continue, I should note that there was no parking on the very narrow one-way street outside the store. We were located on what was the equivalent of a street mall that allowed traffic to run down it. Anyone even remotely familiar with the area was well aware that parking on this particular street practically guaranteed that you were going to get a ticket, but apparently this guy parked right in front of the store.

"I shouldn't have to pay this! I *had* to come here to return those shoes! Now, it's going to cost me forty dollars!" The manager and I just looked at him blankly, both amazed at his self-entitled logic and at a loss as to what he expected us to do about it. Did he really think we would take responsibility for his poor judgment? As if we had somehow forced him to park illegally.

Calmly, our DM spoke up. "Let me see that, buddy."

The man handed him the orange envelope. "See! It cost me forty dollars to come here today!"

What the DM did next was unreal. He took the envelope to the register, rang up a "paid out" for $40, put the cash inside and handed it back to the man. "You're all set, buddy. Have a great afternoon."

Satisfied, the man took back the envelope and left.

No sooner was he out the door, than the manager spoke up. "Are you nuts?"

"Hey, he's going to remember that we went above and beyond," the DM retorted. "That's what it's all about. Creating memorable moments. I guarantee you he'll tell all his friends that story. He'll be back."

The manager knew better than to beat his head against crazy corporate philosophy, so he just chuckled and said, "You're sick."

At the time, I couldn't believe that someone who had risen to the level of district manager could be so naïve about human nature. Not only did the guy cost us a pair of shoes *and* $40, but I never saw him in the store again and I doubt if he ever came back. If he did tell his friends about the incident, I assure you it wasn't in a flattering way. If he retold the story at all it was as a testament to his ability to get what he wanted, not to regale his friends with the tale of the magnanimous shoe salesman.

What a horrible message to send. Now the next time this guy feels like parking on the statehouse lawn while he does his shopping, he's going to march to the last store he visited and demand they pay for his ticket. Of course he won't get the same result, but now that clerk has to give him his rude awakening because we shirked the responsibility.

When it's your turn, do the right thing.

CHILDREN: WHAT YOU CAN BE ANGRY ABOUT

For the record, I'd like to point out that I have two young children and I am a stay-at-home dad, so I'm not ignorant of the challenges presented by raising kids. My children are not always perfect little angels, so I don't expect anyone else's kids to be either.

It's easy to criticize the way people raise their kids when you don't have any. What may seem like abhorrent behavior to someone without children will be understood as perfectly normal to a mother of three. So if you're not a parent, you may be confused when a coworker or customer rebukes you for complaining about the behavior of children in your store. It may astonish you that anyone would defend the little monsters running amok through your aisles.

What you have to understand is parents will always side with other parents (customer or coworker) when it comes to unfair comments about children. However, parents will usually acknowledge or at least ignore legitimate criticism. The trick is to know what's appropriate to scorn.

The following is a list of legitimate reasons to be upset at the parents of unruly children in your store.

Chew on this!

Babies and toddlers chew on things to comfort themselves as part of their normal developmental process. When they're deprived of something to chew on for long periods of time, they often become irritable and start to cry.

Ideally, a parent will bring along a toy or a pacifier when they take their infant shopping to keep them happy. Of course, it's easy to forget little things during the hustle and bustle of the day, so it's not uncommon for a parent to show up at a store and get their child buckled into the shopping cart before realizing that his or her binky has been forgotten. I've found myself in that unfortunate position several times, so I completely sympathize.

What I *don't* sympathize with is how some parents think it's okay to grab a toy off the shelf, let their kid suck on it for forty-five minutes, and then not buy it. Just because they forgot their baby's nukie or na-na doesn't give them the right to destroy merchandise. Either they purchase whatever they gave the kid to chew on or they leave when the baby gets upset. Why should the store suffer for their mistake?

It is completely okay to be upset about this behavior, however there's not much you can do about it. Insisting that the customer pay for the item is a waste of time. Your manager isn't going to go through the hassle of trying to make that happen. But you can definitely be irked about it.

What would be really hilarious is if you were to give each of the items the parent was buying a great big lick before bagging it and say, "You don't mind if I put some spit on your things now, do you?"

But don't do that. You'd get fired and probably arrested.

The lady is going to yell at you!

Threatening your children through the sales associates is not cool. Once I actually had a woman scare her child into staying close to her by pointing at me and saying, *"That man's going to get you!"* Yeah, nothing like teaching your kids that the employees at the local craft store are a bunch of psychopaths ready to pounce on any children who get out of line. How do they discipline their kids when there's no handy stranger nearby to scare them with? *"I'm calling that guy from Toys "R" Us to come kick your ass if you don't clean up your room!"*

It's perfectly normal to be miffed when parents do this. A fun way to turn the tables on a parent who does this is to act super bubbly and kid friendly. Say something like, "Oh, I would never do that! He's such a cutie! How could anyone yell at him! Hey buddy, how old are you?"

Ironically, this may actually accomplish what the parent wanted in the first place. Children usually flee from super chatty adults.

Wee! These shelves are great for climbing!

Whenever a child does something in a store that could get them hurt, damages merchandise, or seriously disrupts other customers, it is the parent's responsibility to step in and take control of the situation. If they shirk that responsibility, then they shouldn't be surprised when an employee takes control of the situation for them.

I've rescued unsupervised three-year-olds from the tops of twenty-foot movable stairs. I've broken up eight-year-olds having sword fights with rolls of Christmas wrapping paper. I've interrupted games of hide-and-seek and put an end to free-for-all "merchandise fights." When parents leave their kids to endanger themselves or wreck the place, you have every right to be upset and intervene.

I think every retail store should staff a child psychology expert like that lady from *Supernanny*. Her job would entail cornering unruly kids and telling them, "Your behavior is unacceptable!" in a British accent. She'd cart bad children off to the stockroom where there would be a row of "naughty mats" and "time-out chairs." Then, before they were allowed to make their purchase, she'd force the parents to watch a surveillance video of the incident and lecture them on how to control their kids.

I can dream, can't I?

Displacer spawn

When I was a kid, I would find some toy in the grocery store and beg my mom to buy it for me. She would say no and tell me to put it back where I found it. If I tried ditching the item in some random place, she would catch me and make sure I brought it back to its proper location. Now that I'm grown up and have kids, I teach my children using the same technique.

It's natural for kids to try skipping steps because they don't think about the consequences of their actions. That's why you need to tell kids not to litter or play with matches. Children also have naturally short attention spans, so you have to teach by constantly reinforcing and repeating the lessons you want them to learn until they get it . . . or until they turn eighteen and you can kick them out.

Adults on the other hand, *are* aware of the consequences of their actions. They know that when their kid tosses some item where it doesn't belong an employee is going to have to pick it up. If they don't care, their kids will grow up not caring, too. I've actually seen parents take the toy their kids are begging for and ditch it themselves.

Displacers beget displacers. There's nothing you can do about it, but you definitely don't have to like it.

Just once, I'd like to find out where a displacer lives, break into their house when they're not home, and toss the place. Not to steal or break anything—just to make a big mess for them to clean up when they got home. It would almost be worth the certain jail time if I actually waited for them to return, so I could see the look on their displacing faces.

"Who's doing recovery now, bee-otch?"

FAUX EMPATHY: PRETENDING YOU CARE

I'd like to offer an easy little trick that can save you a lot of strife.

Often customers will whine to you about things that they know full well you don't have control over—like the prices, or the merchandise selection, or the parking conditions. These are complainers in the making. They haven't graduated to full "complainer" status, but they're testing the waters.

As with full-blown complainers, the best way to get rid of them is by agreeing with their complaint, but you don't have to put on any great theatrics. Just give them a bit of "faux empathy." Put simply, faux empathy is a quick and seemingly genuine acknowledgment of a customer's complaint without any commitment of lengthy dialogue to back it up. As long as you act like you're both on the same team, and sound sincere, it'll work like a charm.

The next time you get some vapid complaint, try concurring, with one of these faux empathy phrases.

- "I know. It's awful isn't it?"
- "Yeah, that's how they get you."
- "You're right, it is stupid."

- "I know, but what can you do?"
- "That's corporate America for you."

Guaranteed to stop any argument dead in its tracks.

THE CUSTOMER IS ALWAYS RIGHT

One of the many retailers I've worked for once had a motivational speaker give a presentation at one of our sales meetings. Part of his presentation was devoted to defending the credo "the customer is always right."

"Of course, the customer isn't *always* right," he explained. "Nobody is *always* right. But whenever there's a disagreement, the customers always *perceive* themselves as right. Even if you win the argument, you lose the customer—because in their minds, they're being treated unfairly. Once a customer perceives a retailer as unfair, they won't give them any more of their business.

"As salespeople, you need to ask yourselves a question—do you want to make money, or do you want to be right?"

I think this pretty well sums up the way most retailers think. I also think this pretty well sums up what's wrong with retail in general.

This penny-wise and pound-foolish interpretation of the infamous philosophy has done nothing but create an ever-growing sense of entitlement among consumers. Society has become so confident that retailers will cave in to their every unreasonable demand that they are not shy at all about abusing them at every turn.

Consumers routinely expect retailers to refund or replace merchandise they've carelessly broken, honor expired coupons, change prices to match their budget, submit to their every unrealistic expectation, and let them treat their employees like indentured servants. What's sad is that retail workers are so accustomed to this way of thinking that they don't even put up a fight anymore. It's second nature for them to let the customers get away with murder. Abuse isn't only tolerated—it's expected.

Recently while in the supermarket, my five-year-old daughter was fooling around and accidentally knocked a bottle of grape soda off one of the shelves. The bottle hit the floor and burst open, spilling fizzy purple liquid everywhere. Embarrassed, I scolded my daughter, alerted one of the employees to the mess, then waited until someone arrived to clean it up. The kid who showed up with the mop was very nice, but when I insisted on paying for the soda he looked at me like I had two heads.

"Oh, you don't have to pay for it," he said dismissively. "Don't worry about it."

"No," I told him. "I insist. My daughter broke it, so I should pay for it."

I took the empty bottle to the counter with me and made sure the girl rang it in. I used the consequences of having to pay for what we had broken as a lesson for my daughter not to fool around in the store.

"Charlotte, when you break something that doesn't belong to you, you have to pay for it," I explained to her. "That's why you need to behave in the store. This time it was only $1.20, but what if you had knocked over something that cost $100 . . . or $1,000? We don't have that kind of money to throw away."

Now she's a lot more careful when we go places. The negative consequence of her bad behavior helped her learn to be more responsible.

This may seem obvious to most, but why isn't it obvious to retailers? Why should their customers bother following the rules when there are no consequences for *not* following them? Customers who voluntarily follow the rules are only punishing themselves, while the customers who abuse the system and behave badly get everything they want.

Unreasonable customers are rewarded. Reasonable customers get the shaft. Logic dictates that perpetuating such a system will eventually generate more bad customers than good—at which point I believe the system will start eating itself and ultimately collapse.

I for one am glad that I won't be there when the spoiled children of retail collectively rise up and beat their proverbial parents to death with an aluminum bat.

NO PROBLEM. I'LL MAKE SURE IT GETS DONE.

WHO WAS THAT?

CORPORATE. THAT GUY YOU DENIED A REFUND TO YESTERDAY CALLED THEM. THEY'RE MAKING US GIVE HIM HIS MONEY BACK.

WHAT?! THEY'RE LETTING THAT JERK RETURN SOFTWARE THAT HE INSTALLED ON HIS COMPUTER?! WHY ARE THEY LETTING HIM GET AWAY WITH THAT?!

HE SAID YOU WERE RUDE TO HIM AND HE THREATENED TO NEVER SHOP HERE AGAIN.

OF COURSE THEY DIDN'T BOTHER GETTING MY SIDE OF THE STORY! I CAN'T THINK OF ANYTHING MORE INSULTING!

THEY ALSO WANT YOU TO APOLOGIZE.

www.COOPERSRETAILBLOG.COM

© 2007 Norman Feuti, Dist. by King Features Syndicate, Inc.

APOLOGIZE?! ARE THEY OUT OF THEIR FREAKIN' MINDS?!

CORPORATE TAKES CUSTOMER SERVICE VERY SERIOUSLY.

THEY TAKE IT TOO FAR! IT'S BAD ENOUGH THAT THEY'RE CAVING IN TO THAT JERK, BUT IF THEY THINK I'M GOING TO APOLOGIZE FOR DEFENDING A STORE POLICY THAT THEY DON'T HAVE THE SPINE TO ENFORCE, THEY HAVE ANOTHER THINK COMING!

IF YOU AGREE WITH THAT INSANITY, THEN YOU APOLOGIZE! I'M WASHING MY HANDS OF IT!

GEEZ, FINE. I HAVE NO PROBLEM DOING THE PROFESSIONAL THING.

SO, WHEN YOU GIVE HIM HIS REFUND, TELL HIM YOU'RE VERY SORRY FOR THE MISUNDERSTANDING ... AND BE SINCERE, OR I'LL WRITE YOU UP.

www.COOPERSRETAILBLOG.COM

© 2007 Norman Feuti, Dist. by King Features Syndicate, Inc.

CHAPTER 7

The Products

There is such a large variety of products to be bought and sold in the world that it would be impossible to cover them all. Luckily I don't have to, because all retailers tend to think of their merchandise in the same way. Whether they're selling jeans, computers, or Rubik's Cubes, retailers all see their individual wares as generic "products" that affect the bottom line in either a positive or negative way.

The buyers in your corporate office perceive the products you sell in much the same way that Neo sees things inside *The Matrix*. What you see as a shovel, the buyers see as a glowing set of numbers and code indicating the object's profit margin, demographic appeal, and emotional marketability.

What you sell makes no real difference. Any retailer you work for is going to have the same attitude toward their products.

FEIGNING PRODUCT KNOWLEDGE

Sooner or later a customer is going to ask you a question about the merchandise that you can't answer. How often this happens depends largely on whether your employer has bothered to teach you anything about the products you sell. If you work in a specialty store selling something like computers or jewelry, you probably will have been given some education on the items you stock. If you work in a big box store selling everything under the sun, you've more than likely been left to figure everything out on your own.

Even when you are somewhat knowledgeable about a product, certain customers will expect you to know every asinine piece of nugatory information about the merchandise. They'll ask questions like "What kind of machine were these yo-yos made on?" or "What temperature do they kiln these coffee cups at?" They'll act as if these ridiculous queries are absolutely make or break, and treat you like some kind of half-ass loser if you can't provide an answer.

Regardless of its validity, you are eventually going to be posed with a product question you don't have the answer to. When this happens, you have two choices.

1. You can admit your ignorance and prepare to be reproached for your lack of knowledge.
2. Pretend you know what you're talking about and hope not to get called on your bullshit.

Neither choice is all that attractive, but with option 2 you at least have a fighting chance to avoid being unfairly scorned.

Notes on Lying

When faced with a question like "Is this safe for babies?" or "What kind of voltage can this thing withstand?" you can't just make something up. You obviously don't want to lie in situations where it could have serious negative consequences to the consumer. If you don't know the answer to a serious question, you have to bite the bullet and confess your lack of knowledge.

On the other hand, when customers ask you questions about the products that are trivial, ridiculous, or otherwise non-issues, lying is the way to go. Inane questions like "How long will these crayons last?" should be answered in an authoritative fashion with whatever big, fat whopper you can come up with on the fly.

"Under average use, you'll get two to three years out of a box, but heavy coloring can reduce that to as little as fourteen months."

I once had a customer ask me what kind of "gription" a particular pair of boots had. Without hesitation, I told him that they had a gription rating of eight. He accepted that answer and seemed genuinely impressed with the rating.

Face-Saving Tips

Even when you're forced to admit that you don't know anything about a specific product, it is sometimes possible to save face and avoid getting berated. The next time you're faced with a difficult product question, try one of these face-saving techniques.

It's New

Sometimes you can turn the negative of your unfamiliarity with the merchandise into a positive by claiming that the product in question is new. Tell them the item just came in and the "product spec sheet" hasn't arrived yet, or there's been a mix-up and the product was delivered before the vendor was scheduled to train the store employees. Not only will this excuse your lack of knowledge, but it will actually make it seem as though your store normally invests a lot of time schooling the staff.

Of course, spec sheets and vendor training are pure fantasy, but most customers have no idea how retail really works. If they knew all your product knowledge came from reading the side of the boxes, they wouldn't bother to ask you in the first place.

Not My Department

Even if you don't have assigned departments, you can always claim that you're not usually stationed wherever you are as an excuse for not knowing the answer to a question. This is only a stalling tactic until you can find someone who actually knows something about the product, but it's a good way to save face.

If you can't find anyone who knows about the product, just tell the customer that the regular guy/girl will be back on a day you aren't scheduled.

CLEARANCE

Trends come and go. When a product is on the downside of a trend or has simply been replaced by a newer model, retailers mark it down as an added incentive for consumers to purchase it. Getting rid of older merchandise in this way makes room for new products and the cycle repeats itself.

In theory this is a sound system, but poor buying decisions

can create problems. Sometimes the buyers in the corporate office misread a line of code in their *Matrix* vision and get so wrapped up in the numbers and huge profit margins that they misjudge trends or overestimate a product's appeal. No matter how smooth the numbers look, a product is worthless if nobody buys it. If I were able to sell my own poo for $20 a pound my profit margin would be huge, but that doesn't mean I should build a booth on my front lawn and start bagging it up.

When these bad decisions happen too often, stores quickly become inundated with more clearance than they can handle— and, like every other bad decision corporate makes, you and your coworkers at the store level will have to suffer for it.

No Cure for Clearance

Once a store's clearance section gets out of hand, it becomes almost impossible to get rid of. It just decays and mutates, then eventually spreads to other parts of the store until it infects every aisle and end-cap.

The real catch-22 is the harder a store tries to get rid of its clearance, the worse the problem gets. When corporate sees that a store is effectively liquidating clearance, they start sending them junk from *other* stores. Rather than saying, *"Good for store number 627! They got rid of all their clearance!"* they say, *"Wow! Store number 627 is really good at selling crap! Send them more!"*

The more clearance a store gets, the more it's forced to sell. The more it sells, the more discount shoppers it attracts. The more discount shoppers it attracts, the more clearance it sells. The more clearance it sells, the more it gets.

A store that gets stuck in this vicious circle long enough eventually becomes a permanent destination for the entire chain's clearance and turns into an outlet store—a mere shadow of its former glory.

An entire chain that gets stuck in this cycle too long is in even bigger trouble, but we'll talk about that in chapter 17.

Game Time!

Here's a fun game you and your coworkers can play when you unload the shipment. When new products come in, see who can spot the merchandise that will end up getting a was/now sticker in the very near future.

Here's how you play:

When a player spots an item he or she thinks will soon be on the discount shelf, they call out "New clearance!" Whoever calls an item first claims it. The item is then out of play. Each player can only call one item per shipment. Seasonal items do not count.

Scoring

The players score points based on the speed with which their called items hit the clearance aisle.

More than 13 weeks = 0 points
8–12 weeks = 1 point
6–7 weeks = 2 points
4–5 weeks = 3 points
Less than 4 weeks = 5 points

The game takes a long time to play, so a cut-off date should be assigned to tally the scores and select a winner. Anyone who quits or gets fired before the cut-off date is disqualified.

Maintaining the Clearance Section

Maintaining the discount aisle sucks because customers have no respect for clearance. Shoppers pick through clearance the way raccoons rummage through garbage cans. They'll haphazardly toss through all the useless junk to find something they might want, leaving behind a mess for the owners of the trash to clean up.

You may be assigned the thankless and daunting task of maintaining or reorganizing the clearance section in your store at some point. If this happens, you'll be charged with creating an orderly display out of ratty, unrelated items to make them as presentable as possible. The technical term for this is "polishing turds."

When you're handed a can of turd polish, my advice is to do as half-ass a job as possible. If you do too good of a job, the manager is going to make you Captain Clearance and you'll be on permanent crap-shining duty. Having to do it once in a while is one thing, but getting stuck on constant clearance patrol is like being hired to keep a tower of blocks standing in a room full of toddlers.

Nobody has that kind of vigilance or patience.

DAMAGES

Merchandise gets broken all the time. Sometimes products get damaged in shipment, but more often customers break them— either in the store accidentally or when they get home. In the latter case, the customer will frequently pretend the item was damaged out of the box and demand a refund.

Even though the vast majority of damaged products are only dinged in minor cosmetic ways that don't prevent them from functioning properly, most retailers don't make a policy of discounting them. Instead, they favor writing them off as a loss and tossing them in the Dumpster. Then, to ensure that the employees or other industrious individuals don't root through the trash to claim the discarded merchandise for free, these retailers will take the preemptive step of smashing, marring, or defacing the products in some way to make them completely unusable.

This behavior perfectly illustrates the illogical circle of waste and inefficiency that retail giants have forced themselves into. Because of the sheer volume of merchandise they stock and customers they service, huge retail chains end up with a lot of damaged merchandise—it's inevitable. Since the cost required to staff every store in a massive chain with a trained stock manager, equipped with the means to report and apply for credit on damaged items from a myriad of vendors, would far exceed the benefit, it is less costly to throw merchandise away. Besides, a retail giant's merchandise goes through so many hands during its long journey from various factories and distributors in the Far East, over oceans, and through customs, it's nearly impossible to hold the vendor accountable for the condition of a product by the time a stock boy in Iowa unpacks it.

While the owners of a little mom-and-pop store can cut their losses by discounting any damaged merchandise they get stuck with, a big retail chain doesn't have that option. Retail giants have so many employees, they can't know them on a personal level and therefore can't trust them to make decisions when it comes to arbitrarily discounting merchandise. Wal-Mart has well over a million employees. To trust them all with discounting damaged merchandise willy-nilly would be like putting the entire state of Rhode Island on the honor system.

Since the big retail chains can't trust their employees, they have to institute a policy that makes it impossible to claim a discount on merchandise due to damage. The easiest way to do that is to require that all damaged merchandise be thrown away. Of course this leads to the logical conclusion of employees getting supposedly damaged merchandise out of the Dumpster for free, so a further policy has to be instituted requiring all damaged merchandise to be destroyed before being thrown away.

In short, most retail giants have put themselves in a position where any damaged merchandise that can't be sold for 100 percent of the original price has to be cut up, smashed with a hammer, or defaced with spray paint. While this does indeed prevent employees from stealing or discounting merchandise that isn't legitimately broken, it also prevents the retailer from cutting their losses on merchandise that *is* legitimately damaged but still usable.

There isn't anything you can do with this information. I've only included it to educate you so you won't be confused the first time a manager gives you a vase with a small chip in it, then hands you a hammer and a pair of safety glasses.

The Cover-up

Like all of a retail corporation's deficiencies and weaknesses, the insane destruction of barely damaged merchandise has to be covered up with a lie. Here are some common lies that retail giants feed their employees to make their wasteful practices seem justified.

1. If we made a habit of marking down damaged merchandise, it would only encourage customers to break things in minor ways to get a discount.
2. The vendors credit us for everything we destroy.
3. We don't want to soil our good reputation by selling substandard merchandise.

For fun, you can ask your manager why you destroy the damaged merchandise instead of marking it down to see if he or she will regurgitate one of those three lines. Some savvy managers will tell you the truth, but most will lie to you willingly. Retailers think if they admit that a policy exists primarily to prevent the employees from stealing that it's going to hurt their morale. It probably would, but feeding the employees illogical bullshit doesn't instill them with confidence either. I'd rather have my employees think I was distrustful than think I was insane.

We'll delve deeper into the corporate psyche in chapter 13. For now, just keep in mind that most illogical policies are designed to keep you from ripping off your employer.

CHAPTER 8

The Stockroom

P eople who have never worked behind a counter tend to have idealistic or downright fantastic misconceptions about the way retail works. So to understand why customers act the way they do, you have to get inside their heads.

When it comes to your stockroom, the customer imagines an organized storage facility with a clearly labeled space for each item the store carries. They presume that the employees restock the sales floor from the stockroom, and that the stockroom gets restocked when you receive a shipment. In short, the customer thinks your stockroom is a magical mini-warehouse.

Of course in reality, the stockroom is just where merchandise is received and unpacked before being taken directly to the sales floor. The constant effort to move every last bit of merchandise out of the back room before the next enormous shipment arrives means that there is almost never any merchandise left in the back room that isn't represented on the sales floor. What little overstock does remain in the stockroom is all kept in nondescript boxes labeled with vague codes placed randomly on unmarked shelves. Some of the managers and the people who run stock sort of know what's in those boxes, but the average employee doesn't have much of a clue.

It's this basic misconception that causes a lot of grief for retail employees. When a customer insists that you check to see if you have any more blue vases in the back, they're imagining a straightforward procedure. They think that all you have to do is go to the "blue vases" shelf in the stockroom and see if there's anything there. What they don't know is that if you *were* to entertain the very slim possibility that a case of blue vases was overlooked, you'd have to spend hours opening every box in the back room trying to locate it.

Although I have a feeling that even if the customers *were* aware that you'd have to search vainly through a sea of identical boxes just to be absolutely positive that you didn't have what they wanted, they'd probably still expect you to do it.

PRETEND CHECKING

Some customers won't take no for an answer . . . actually, in my experience *most* customers won't take no for an answer. No matter how emphatic or sure you are that a particular item is out of stock, they just won't be satisfied until you go check to see if there's any more "in the back."

The exchange usually goes something like this:

CUSTOMER: "Excuse me, do you have any more of these candle holders?"

SALESPERSON: "No, I'm sorry, that's the last one."

CUSTOMER: "*Sigh*. You don't have *any* more?"

SALESPERSON: "No, sorry."

CUSTOMER: "None at all?"

SALESPERSON: "No."

CUSTOMER: "Not even in the back?"

SALESPERSON: "No, I'm afraid not. We'll probably get more in next week though."

CUSTOMER: "No, I need it today."

SALESPERSON: "Hmm. Well, sorry about that."

CUSTOMER: "So, you're sure that you don't have any?"

SALESPERSON: "Yes."

CUSTOMER: "Because I only need *one* more."

SALESPERSON: ". . . "

CUSTOMER: "Could you at least go check in the back, just to make sure?"

SALESPERSON: "*Sigh* Yeah, I'll be right back . . . *grumble, grumble.*"

This exchange will repeat itself several times a day during your retail career, so get used to it. Even if you tell the customer that you just checked on the very same item for somebody else and know for a fact that you don't have any in the stockroom, they'll still look at you skeptically and insist that you go check anyway.

This attitude is partially due to the common misconception described at the beginning of this chapter, but it is also partially due to the unfair, negative stereotype that retail employees suffer from. Most customers think all retail employees are lazy good-for-nothings, so they assume that you're lying to avoid a walk to the stockroom.

In any event, this exchange almost always ends in "pretend checking." Pretend checking is when you go to the stockroom and pretend to look for merchandise that you know isn't there just to appease a stubborn customer. You walk in the back, wait for what would seem like an appropriate amount of time to search for something, then head back out to the customer, shaking your head sympathetically.

"Sorry, I looked everywhere and we're completely out."

Finally satisfied, the customer will leave you alone . . . or have you spend the next hour calling every other store in the district to see if they have the item.

One thing that a lot of new retail employees fail to realize is that they can often turn the regular annoyance of pretend checking to their favor. Rather than suffer through the tedious exchange of answering the same question six times before being sent to the stockroom on a faux search, offer to go check the back right off the bat. Not only will you get to take multiple five- and ten-minute breaks throughout the day, but the customer will actually see it as good service. If you're lucky enough to have a break room connected to the stock area, then just head back there for a few minutes. Have a Diet Coke, read a comic book—whatever.

The beauty of pretend checking is that even if a manager catches you, there isn't anything they can really do. Just tell him or her that the customer insisted that you look for merchandise that you know you're out of and you're just killing a few minutes. You can't tell the customer no, and there's no reason to look for what you know doesn't exist, so what can the manager say? Hell, they do it all the time, too.

The real irony is that the customer will interpret your resistance to inefficiently wasting time looking for something that doesn't exist as lazy, while they'll see your immediate offer to go to the stockroom (where you text a friend from your cell phone or shoot the breeze with whoever is on break) as excellent customer service.

Note: Whenever you get caught goofing off in the stockroom, you might be able to get out of it by using the "pretend checking" excuse.

MAKING FUN OF THE CUSTOMERS

Outside of pretending to look for merchandise, the stockroom is also good for venting your frustrations when customers do stupid or outrageous things. The stockroom is one of the few sacred areas where you can speak freely, so use it to blow off steam.

Here's a story that illustrates just how valuable the stockroom is for this purpose.

Binoculars for Sebastian

Once, while I was working for that same "educational" gift store where the skeleton T-shirt misspelling incident took place,

I was flagged down by a woman who wanted to see the binoculars that we had in a locked display case. She was with her son who appeared to be around ten years old. The boy hovered nearby looking at this and that and seemed completely disinterested in the binoculars.

"I'm looking for a pair of binoculars for my son to take with him on our vacation to Europe," she said.

"Wow, Europe," I said enviously. "That sounds exciting."

"Well, we've been before," she said dismissively. "We were looking at the binoculars they have in Brookstone, but they all looked too big. I want something small that he can carry around without getting tired, but I don't want anything cheap."

"Okay, well we carry three different models," I said opening the case. "This first one is fairly simple. It's twenty-five dollars and has a magnification of . . ."

"I said I don't want anything cheap," she squawked, cutting me off rudely.

Mrs. Europe-Is-No-Big-Whoop was pissing me off in fairly short order, so I decided to cut to the most expensive pair and keep my patter brief. "Well, this is the best pair we have. It has a zoom feature that gives you a magnification range of seven to twenty-one times. It's a hundred and forty dollars."

"Seven to twenty-one times what?" she asked in a tone that suggested there was no way she could possibly guess what I was referring to.

"Normal vision," I replied.

"I don't get it," she said, confused. "What does that mean?"

This honestly didn't faze me much. In the great pantheon of stupid questions, this hardly made the list, so I was able to remain patient without much effort. "Twenty-one times magnification just means that objects viewed through the binoculars will look twenty-one times closer than they would normally. Something twenty-one feet away will look like it's only one foot away."

"So you can only see things that are twenty-one feet away?" she asked, unimpressed.

"No, it means that *anything* you look at will look twenty-one times closer. Something that is 2,100 feet away will look like it's only 100 feet away. Something that's 21,000 feet away will look like it's only 1,000 feet away. Of course the farther away something is, the less difference it's going to make, but you get the picture."

Her face told me that she didn't get the picture at all. "Well, is that magnification good? Will he be able to see things through it?"

"Realistically that's about the best you'll get out of a small pair of binoculars," I said, "You can find a much more powerful pair, but they'd be larger than you want."

"You're avoiding my question," she snapped curtly.

This was strike three and I felt my patience starting to slip away. "Yes. It's a good magnification and he'll be able to see *things* through it," I said flatly. Trying to divert her from making another rude comment that might throw me over the edge, I added. "Would your son like to look through them? See what he thinks?"

Thankfully, she took me up on the offer. "Sebastian, come look at these for a minute."

"Okay," the boy said, without looking up from the book he was thumbing through. He casually tossed it onto a fixture that it didn't belong on and joined his mother's side. The lack of a reprimand hardly surprised me at this point.

"Go out in the hallway and look through these, honey." She handed the boy the binoculars and he did as she asked. Sebastian scanned the mall with the binoculars quickly, then came back in and handed them back to his mother without a word. He quickly returned to the book he had been looking at earlier.

The woman put her hands on her hips comically and let out a playful laugh that made me want to punch her in the face. "Sebastian! What did you think of them, sweetie?" she gushed with mock exasperation.

Sebastian couldn't be bothered to look at her. "They're fine," he said, annoyed.

Her brow furrowed. Unbelievably, she seemed concerned by

his irritation, rather than pissed, like a normal parent. "Well, were they too heavy, honey?" she asked gently.

Sebastian shrugged his shoulders.

She turned back to me. "Well, how heavy are these? I don't want him to get tired carrying them. Europe's a big place."

God, I wanted this to be over. Forget the Europe comment, the lady was asking me how heavy the pair of binoculars she had in her hand was. In the real world, if anyone picked up an object, then asked someone else how heavy it was, they wouldn't be able to escape ridicule. You couldn't pick up a brick, then ask your buddies, "Hey guys, how heavy is this brick I'm holding?" without somebody calling you a moron. Only a customer could get away with that level of idiocy without consequence.

In my mind, I let out a heavy sigh. "I'd have to guess it weighs less than a pound."

"I don't want you to guess," she chided. "I want to know exactly!"

Must. Not. Kill.

This time I let out a real sigh. "Well, let's look at the box." I grabbed the box out of the display case and thankfully it listed the weight on the side in ounces. Like most people, I don't use weights and measures on a regular basis, so I had to think it through for a second. "It's twelve ounces, and there's . . . sixteen ounces in a pound, right?"

With a smug look, the woman raised her eyebrow and called to her son without breaking eye contact with me, "Sebastian, how many ounces are in a pound?"

"Sixteen," he said without hesitation. As he said it, she raised her eyebrow a little higher and smirked a little deeper as if to say, "Even my ten-year-old son knows how many ounces are in a pound, stupid."

In my fifteen-plus years in retail, this is the closest I've come to flipping out on a customer without actually doing it. I've had customers who were worse that I did flip out on, but this lady was right on the threshold. Patiently putting up with her litany of moronic questions and condescending attitude only to have her imply that her ten-year-old brat was smarter than me was my absolute limit. If she had said anything else, I would have lost it.

I just stared at her blankly, trying to contain my rage. My face must have given it away, because she lost the smirk pretty quickly and handed the binoculars back to me.

"Um, well I'm still not sure," she said timidly, the tone she had been using suddenly absent.

I tossed the binoculars back in the case with a clatter and locked the door loudly. "Yeah, well, when you make up your mind, just let someone know," I said brusquely and made a bee-line for the back room.

I remained in the stockroom for about an hour. I don't re-member or care if anyone else ended up selling her the binoc-ulars, nor do I care if Sebastian's delicate little genius body got all tuckered out on their ho-hum nth trek across Europe. What I do remember is reenacting the scenario over and over again for my coworkers and doing the most unflattering im-pression of Mrs. How-Heavy-Is-the-Object-I'm-Holding I could muster.

I made it my sole purpose in life to make fun of her for the next week and I felt better because of it.

The cathartic benefit of making fun of customers in the stockroom is undeniable. Without it, the cumulative effects of 1,001 sucky customers would eventually push you over the edge.

The stockroom is the perfect place for taking lemons and turn-ing them into lemonade . . . or, I guess more appropriately, it's the perfect place for letting your hate flow to make yourself feel better.

Whatever. Same thing.

LADDERS ARE FOR ROOKIES

If you're new to retail, you'll soon discover that much of your job involves getting things down from high places. Not only in the stockroom, but on the sales floor as well.

Your instincts will rightly tell you that you should use a ladder for such tasks, but in retail, ladders are always in short supply. Inevitably you're going to be given a job that requires a ladder, only to find that both of them are being used (and heavily guarded) by your coworkers. You can always try to borrow a ladder from a coworker with the promise that you'll "bring it right back," but that's a crapshoot at best. Any employee who is lucky enough to have control of a ladder probably won't be too keen on giving it up. Any experienced retail drone knows that loaning a coworker your ladder is like letting a crackhead borrow your stereo—while it's theoretically possible that you'll get it back, you really shouldn't count on it.

Your boss will never accept your inability to commandeer a ladder as a legitimate excuse for failing to get your work done, so it's best not to rely on them at all. In retail, the ladder is a crutch that you have to rid yourself of.

Here are some alternate (and completely unsafe) methods for getting things down from high shelves.

Prod and Catch

When the out-of-reach item in question isn't fragile and is positioned near the edge of a shelf, you can use this method to retrieve it. Simply grab a broom, mop, or any other polelike object to prod the box or item repeatedly from the side or underneath until you have coaxed it off of the shelf.

If the item is light, you can ditch your broom just as the box teeters over the edge of the shelf and catch it before it hits the floor. If the box is heavy, simply move out of the way and let it fall. Hopefully in the latter case, the majority of the merchandise inside will withstand the impact undamaged.

Crouching Tiger, Hidden Dragon

The advanced stocker can scale shelving like Chow Yun Fat or Jackie Chan to obtain the merchandise he or she needs.

Using earth magic and the spirit of the wind, a seasoned retail employee can practically walk on air. I once witnessed an experienced stock boy use an unstable mountain of boxes as a stairway to reach a shelf at ceiling height. He did it in seconds without disturbing a thing. It was nothing short of magical.

It kind of undermined the sense of wonder in the feat when he got to the top and carelessly kicked the huge boxes he wanted over the edge, letting them drop thirty feet onto the concrete floor . . . but still.

Surrogate Ladders

When shelf climbing and prodding aren't options, you might have to find some other object you can stand on to reach what you want. Here are some objects commonly found in a retail setting that may do the trick.

- Inverted trashcan (remove garbage first!)
- Floor samples or merchandise (chairs, stools, tables, etc. . . .)
- Dolly or pallet jack
- Coworkers

Of course your employer would forbid you from setting yourself up to sustain a crippling injury by following any of this advice, but they're not going to offer you any safe alternatives either. They'll just insist that you complete your work the right way, knowing full well that the only way to get things done in the horribly inefficient system they've created is by breaking the rules.

As long as corporate tells you to be safe, they can save money on extra ladders and force you to make your own tough choices.

CHAPTER 9

Break Time

Depending on what store you work for, you may be allowed to take a break at some point during your shift. Retail breaks are usually unpaid and range between fifteen minutes and half an hour depending on the length of your shift on any given day.

Regular employees have strictly scheduled breaks that they usually get to take uninterrupted, while managers and supervisors rarely get to sit down for more than a few minutes at a time without getting paged to handle a customer complaint, take a phone call, or turn a key somewhere. Management breaks will be scheduled as a matter of formality and company policy, but will never actually occur at the time they are supposed to. A supervisor's break is so amorphous and chopped up that it usually takes him or her an entire shift to get in a full half-hour's worth of sporadic seven-minute lunch breaks.

Whether you're a member of management or a regular employee, this chapter will tell you what to expect at lunch time and offer you tips on how to maximize your break.

LOCATION, LOCATION, LOCATION

The first thing to consider when getting ready for your break is where you will take it. If you take your break in the store, you'll obviously have to find a place out of sight of the customers. If you're lucky, your store will have a break room with snack machines, a fridge, and a disgustingly filthy microwave. If you're unlucky, you'll have to pull up a box in the dusty stockroom.

If you work in a mall, you will have the option of taking your break in the food court, but I would advise against it. While you'll often travel to the food court to get your lunch, you'll probably find it unpleasant eating there—especially on the weekends when it's crowded. If you find an uncomfortable, wobbly seat at all, it's going to be next to a gaggle of little kids getting barked at by their parents to sit still, or a group of giggly fourteen-year-olds whose vapid conversation you'll be forced to listen to. If you're female, there's also a 70 percent chance that you'll be leered at by some lone weirdo while you eat. My advice is to spend as little time in the food court as possible.

If you're a manager, you have the option of taking your break in the office. If it's a real office with four walls and a door, you'll get to enjoy a little privacy, but more than likely the "office" in your store is just a thrift store–bought teacher's desk shoved in a dark corner of the stockroom somewhere—the unused surface of which is barely sufficient to hold your Whopper Jr. and fries.

EXIT STRATEGIES

When break time rolls around, you're going to need to get from the sales floor to the time clock in the back room. This may sound simple, but if you don't have an exit strategy you're going to get buttonholed by a customer who wants help before you can reach the stockroom.

A single customer can potentially delay your break by as much as an hour, or, if you're a manager, force you to forfeit your break entirely in some cases. Even if that single customer doesn't detain you for long, every minute you help them increases the likelihood that a second customer will approach and wait to solicit your help the moment you're finished with the first. Not to mention that the help these customers need will likely take you even farther away from the "employees only" door than you were in the first place, putting you in an even worse position for departure.

There are several ways to decrease the likelihood of getting collared by a customer. Be sure to take the following precautions before and during your attempt to leave the sales floor.

1. Remove Your Nametag/Apron

The first and most basic step you should take to increase your odds of getting off of the sales floor unobstructed is to remove anything that identifies you as an employee. If you're unfortunate enough to have to wear a uniform or polo shirt branded with your store name, consider wearing a plain T-shirt beneath your uniform or keeping a baggy sweater hidden beneath the register somewhere.

If you can't be easily identified as an employee, your odds of safe passage increase dramatically.

2. Choose an Escape Route

When you've discarded all of your corporate branding, do a quick scan to find the path of least customer resistance. The fewer customers you pass, the better your odds.

The most common mistake rookies make is to take the main aisle to the back room. While this is usually the shortest route from the registers to the stockroom, it is also the most likely place to get flagged down by a customer. The main aisle is a highway for lazy shoppers. The customers who can't be bothered to look for the merchandise they want always stay on the main aisle and grab the first employee they see. Then they make the employee lead them by the hand to each and every item on their list.

Avoid the main aisles in general if you can.

3. Avoid Eye Contact

If a customer is unsure whether you work in the store, they'll be reluctant to ask you if you're an employee for fear of being embarrassed. Of course when you're pricing merchandise while standing on a ladder wearing a nametag and apron, they won't hesitate to ask . . . but that's just the way of the customer.

If you make eye contact with a customer who is on the cusp of asking you if you're an employee, it will give them just enough encouragement to do it, so keep your eyes on the prize or glued to the floor.

4. Act Like a Customer

Another mistake rookies make on their way to the back room is that they walk too fast and purposefully. If you want the customers to think that you're just another shopper, you have to act like one of them. Saunter casually and be sure to look around at the merchandise with an air of mild interest and discovery as you go. If necessary, you can complete the illusion by picking up an item, then putting it back in the wrong place.

Remember, customers can smell fear. Don't undermine your own efforts by making a beeline for the stockroom at mach speed—you'll just be calling attention to yourself.

5. The Rule of Three

Despite your best efforts of stealth, you're going to get the occasional customer who recognizes you or just senses that you're an employee. If you've followed all the rules up to this point, you still have the "rule of three" as a last chance to avoid having a customer delay your break.

The rule is simple. If you can make it into the stockroom before the customer says "Excuse me" three times, you're off the hook. When a customer makes you as an employee, just keep moving and act as if you don't hear them. If they say "Excuse me" a second time, increase your speed slightly without being obvious about it. If you haven't made it through the stockroom doors before the last "Excuse me!" you have to stop.

Three seems to be the magic number by which one's suspension of disbelief is severed. The customer might buy that you didn't hear them the first two times they called, but they'll never believe that you didn't hear them yelling "*Excuse me!*" the third time as you shove an old woman out of the way and bolt through the stockroom doors.

If you ignore the "rule of three," you're taking your chances.

DOUBLE STANDARDS: A SHORT STORY

I used to work as a cashier for an arts-and-crafts supply store. The store was located in a strip mall and since there was no place on the plaza to get food, I would often drive across the street to Wal-Mart and grab something from the McDonald's that was inside. Even though it was just across the street, getting through the busy intersection and parking took up a good portion of my break, so I never had a moment to waste when I decided to do it.

One hot summer day I had a hankering for a Crispy Chicken meal, so when it came time for my half-hour break, I punched out and headed across the street post haste. By the time I had gotten back, I had a little over fifteen minutes left on my break. To save time I would usually just eat in my car, but this particular day was sweltering and my car had been baking in the parking lot all morning, so I chose to go inside and eat in the break room.

No sooner did I get inside the store than a woman stopped me and desperately asked, "Do you work here?" Oddly, she was perceptive enough to know that I was an employee even though I wasn't wearing my apron. Yet she wasn't keen enough to be tipped off by the McDonald's bag and large soft drink I was holding, or my recent entrance, to suspect that I wasn't on the clock.

"Um . . . yeah, but I'm on break," I said.

She threw her arms in the air melodramatically. "But I can't find anyone else to help me in here!"

The store was unusually busy that day, so I assessed that she was probably being truthful. Not that I thought that was my problem exactly, but I figured the quickest way to get her away from me was to point her in the right direction.

"Well, what are you looking for?" I asked.

"I already know what I want," she huffed. "I need a seven-foot ficus tree, but they're all displayed out of reach. I need you to get one down for me."

The store stocked artificial ficus trees in large quantities, and to avoid taking up space in the stockroom we displayed the overstock on high shelves around the perimeter of the store. The problem was that on a busy day during a sale, the trees on the floor would sell quicker than our meager staff was able to replenish them, so we'd end up having to drag around a twenty-foot moveable stairway to get them down upon request.

Admittedly, none of this was her fault. A deficiency in the store's system was preventing her from helping herself to a tree, while simultaneously preventing her from finding an employee to get one for her. I understood and sympathized with her dilemma completely, so I figured the least I could do was take a minute to page someone to help her when I got to the break room.

"Okay, I'll page someone to get one down for you," I told her.

"Can't *you* help me?" she whined.

"No, I can't," I said. "I'm on break." I was really starting to get perturbed that she wasn't getting that part.

"Can't you just take your break later?" she asked crassly. "Your food will still be there."

Nothing pisses me off more than when a customer abandons reason in favor of the stereotype that all retail workers are lazy. Why else would she make the automatic assumption that I could take my break whenever I pleased, but was just choosing to use it as an excuse not to help her? Not to mention that I had told her repeatedly that I was already *on* break—not *going* on break—*on* break.

"No, I have to take my break when they tell me to," I said matter-of-factly. "Besides, I'm right in the *middle* of my break. I have fifteen minutes left to eat my food, or else I go without lunch today. I'll get someone else to help you."

Her eyes widened in disbelief and she huffed as though I was being incredibly unreasonable. "It would only take you a minute!"

"I'm off the clock," I said bluntly, trying to drive the point through her thick skull. "I'm not being paid right now, so I'll get someone else to help you."

"Oh, so you're one of those people who won't do anything unless they get paid for it?" she asked snottily. She looked at me with disgust, as if my attitude was exactly what was wrong with the world.

I had to get out of there before this went to a really bad place, so I just said, "Yeah, I'm funny that way," and walked off.

At no other job could an employee conceivably be accused of being lazy if they refused to work for free. But somehow a retail employee is supposed to be *so* subservient and dedicated to customer service that they should sacrifice even their most basic employee rights so some jerk doesn't have to wait a few extra minutes for their fake tree.

It's a basic double standard that exists for retail workers. An office worker who refused to work off the clock would never be treated like some shirking ne'er-do-well, he'd be lauded as a hero for standing up to any corporate snake that tried to impose something so blatantly unfair and illegal. But the retail worker who does the same thing is looked at as a lazy bastard with no commitment to his job.

Likewise, office workers don't get chastised and labeled when they occasionally surf the Internet or gossip on company time, it's just looked at as normal and unavoidable human behavior. But when retail workers get caught talking to each other or laughing, they're scorned and treated like degenerate layabouts.

It's an inequity that I found I could stomach less and less the longer I worked in retail.

Anyway, I never paged anyone to help that lady. Screw her.

PROPAGANDA

Once you've made it to the break room/area in your store, you'll undoubtedly notice a plethora of brightly colored posters covering the walls. Some of those posters will be mandatory displays of state and federal labor laws, but most of them will be propaganda designed by your corporate office.

Retail agitprops generally have a distinctly Orwellian feel, using definitive statements like "Theft Affects Everyone" or "The Customer Always Comes First" in an effort to convince you that you should take your employer's problems to heart—and after reading them every day for months and years, you may find the concepts they exhort starting to make sense to you. Such is the nature of propaganda.

Just remember to take these "informative" posters with a grain of salt. Anything the corporate office bothers to spend money on and distribute is only done out of self-interest, so don't lend them too much credence.

Take "Theft Affects Everyone," for example. The corporate office uses a poster like this to make you feel like your crappy salary and their high prices are somehow a product of your behavior. They're trying to suggest that if you were more diligent in preventing shoplifting, they'd be able to pay you more and make their products more affordable. But think about it—if your store were able to somehow reduce theft to zero percent, do you really think the home office would increase your pay or slash prices? No, it's far more likely that they would use the money you saved them to open another store or raise their own salaries. At best, theft indirectly affects your employer's ability to expand and employ more minimum-wage help, but that wouldn't be likely to motivate you and it's far too wordy for a catch phrase.

Let corporate worry about its own problems. Don't let them snow you into thinking that they're not partially culpable for your apathy. If you don't care about the store's bottom line, it's probably because they haven't given you a good reason to.

Besides, if they could get away with it, they'd hang up signs that said "Unions Eat Babies" and "Overtime Causes High Cholesterol," so it's best not to take them too seriously.

SNACK MACHINES

If your store has a break room, you'll probably have a couple of vending machines from which to grab a quick pick-me-up. For some reason, snack machine technology hasn't improved since the '70s. Vending machines still use the same spinning, curly wire mechanism that snags your bag of Cheetos or M&Ms 15 percent of the time. In an age where we can put a robot on Mars, you'd think they could invent a machine that would dispense snacks without the occasional need to rock it back and forth violently . . . but what do I know?

Anyway, the occasional loss of money isn't something you can avoid, but there's one thing you *can* look out for—the brownies. Don't ever choose a brownie from a vending machine—I guarantee it's hard as a rock. Cookies are hit or miss, but you should avoid them, too, unless you can get a testimonial from a coworker that they're okay. There are plenty of other snacks to watch out for, but baked goods are the most notorious. As a general rule of thumb, any snack in a slot that's full all the way to the back is probably stale or just plain awful.

Another tip: occasionally you'll notice that the snack machine has been refilled with your favorite goody, only to find that it's been put in a slot behind the leftovers of some undesirable candy. This is a scummy though admittedly shrewd tactic on the snack vendor's behalf that you're just going to have to live with. My advice is to take one on the chin once in a while and buy one of the crappy snacks so your coworkers can have access to the good stuff. It's good karma, and hopefully someone will repay the favor for you one day.

TURNING A COAT HANGER
INTO A MAKESHIFT ANTENNA

Back in chapter 4, I alluded to the bent coat hanger you might have seen sticking out of the back of the TV/VCR you watched all those horrible/funny training videos on. If you stick a bent coat hanger into the cable jack of a TV and position it just right, it serves as a makeshift antenna and you can pick up some network stations.

Using the "training monitor" in this way is very much against the rules, so corporate is always sure to toss out the actual antennas before they supply the TVs to the stores. They know this measure doesn't stop anyone from jury-rigging a solution, but they still do it as a symbolic act to make their position clear. Corporate doesn't want your breaks running long because you're glued to a football game or can't tear yourself away from *The King of Queens*. Watching a movie on the VCR is forbidden for the same reason . . . but there's nothing they can throw away to symbolically communicate that, so they just tell you not to.

How clandestine you need to be when watching TV or *Raiders of the Lost Ark* during your break is largely dependent on the "coolness" of your manager and district manager, which should become apparent to you through gossip or firsthand experience within the first couple of months.

Until you know how seriously your employer will view this infraction, it's best to refrain from it altogether.

Note: If video sleeves and a bent coat hanger are left in plain sight for any newbie to see, chances are that nobody at the store level views this extracurricular use of the TV as a big deal.

CHAPTER 10

Etiquette

How Not to Be the One
Everybody Hates

Every job has a few unspoken rules that become understood by the employees through experience—retail is no different. Certain actions and behaviors will be considered unacceptable by your coworkers, and if you break these taboos too frequently you'll soon find yourself the object of everyone's scorn. If you walk into the break room and everyone suddenly stops talking, it's a good bet that you're doing something the rest of the staff considers "not cool."

Here is some advice to follow if you want to prevent your coworkers from occasionally putting together an impromptu hate-fest in your honor.

ANSWERING THE PHONE
In retail, answering the phone is like playing Russian roulette. You always hope it's a coworker looking for their schedule, but you know there's a one in six chance that it will be some pain-in-the-ass customer who wants you to describe the contents of your store in minute detail.

"Hello, Borders? Yes, I was wondering if you could tell me the names of every cookbook you carry? Also, do you have that book that was on Oprah a few years back? It has a blue cover and I think it's about women getting in touch with their feelings."

It's natural to want to avoid the phone like the plague, but if you're the closest one to it when it rings, you have to pick it up—that's the rule. All retail employees have to deal with the same bullshit. You're not special.

If you make a habit of ditching your fair share of the phone load on others, your coworkers will eventually catch on and get even with you. They'll start tricking you into taking the worst calls that pop up and then you'll really be sorry.

"What's that? You'd like someone to smell each scented candle we carry and give you a review over the phone? Sure, let me get our candle expert. Hold on. Hey, Roy, your girlfriend is on line two."

If you know what's good for you, you'll take your lumps as they come like everybody else.

PAGING

If your store is equipped with an intercom to call other employees, for God's sake learn how to use it! There's nothing more grating on the ears than the amplified clatter of some newbie hanging up the phone without turning off the intercom first.

Also, learn how to speak in a clear, audible voice when paging someone. If you're knee-deep in boxes frantically trying to complete some task in the far corner of the stockroom, the last thing you need is to hear what might be your name at the beginning of some garbled incoherency. Then, you have to stop what you're doing and try to find out if, who, and why someone paged you just in case it was something important . . . which it almost never is.

[BEEP]

"Steve zum ernal a bazerub, please. Steve, zum ernal a bazerub."

[CLATTER-CLICK]

When it comes to using the intercom at the end of the night to make the store closing announcements, speaking clearly becomes doubly important. Most customers don't listen to the announcements anyway, but you at least want the few considerate souls who might be wandering the aisles to understand that you're closing in ten minutes.

PAWNING OFF PROBLEM CUSTOMERS AND COMPLAINTS

There's one big rule in retail that you can't break. Once you start helping a customer, you are *stuck* with that customer. No matter what kind of problem they have, or how rude, asinine, or needy they might be, you can't ditch them on a coworker simply to avoid the hassle of dealing with them yourself.

There are only two exceptions to this rule.

1. The Customer Requests to Speak to Somebody Else

If at any time the customer you're helping asks to speak to a manager (or *the* manager if you're already a supervisor) because you can't give them what they want, it is then acceptable to pawn them off. Also, if the customer says something like "Is there somebody else here who knows what they're talking about?" you can legitimately wash your hands of them and recommend them to another employee.

Trying to elicit a request for alternate help from your customer by intentionally acting incompetent is technically legal, but is considered by most to be poor form.

2. Non-Supervisors Can Always Refer Complaints to Managers

If you aren't a supervisor on any level, you can always hand off a customer who has a complaint to a manager. This is always considered acceptable and is even required in some stores.

Pawning off every trivial gripe to a manager in knee-jerk fashion is legal, but again, is considered poor form by most.

> CUSTOMER: *"Excuse me, why do these pillows cost so much?"*
> EMPLOYEE: *"Let me get a manager for you."*

These loopholes are the only two ways you can legitimately pawn off a customer on a coworker, so the better you are at identifying problem customers *before* you get stuck waiting on them, the better off you'll be.

Be sure to go back and study chapter 6 thoroughly if you haven't already. I can't stress that enough. Because when it comes to *avoiding* customers, all bets are off and it's every man for himself. There aren't any rules that say you can't throw a naïve coworker under the bus the moment you spot a kook or a reeker headed your way.

Just divert your eyes, back away silently, and put that less savvy retail worker between you and approaching doom.

CALLING IN SICK

Most jobs offer a number of "personal days" or "sick days" to their employees that they can use to take paid time off when something unexpected comes up, but retail work offers no such luxury. In retail, you can take an unpaid day off if something comes up, but you have to *pretend* to be sick.

While none of your coworkers will think that you should be above faking an illness to get out of work occasionally (because they do it, too), there is a certain protocol that you'll be expected to follow.

1. Have the Common Courtesy to Lie

Even though everybody knows that people aren't really sick half of the time they call out, you still have to put on a show when you do it. Every time you call out, the other employees have to work harder to pick up the slack, so letting on that you weren't really sick before or after the fact is considered extremely rude.

You can't call out sick on Friday night without so much as a fake cough, then gloat about how great the concert was on Saturday morning—that's just a slap in the face. You need to show your coworkers that you respect them by putting on your best sick voice over the phone, and then following up the performance the next day by acting sluggish and wheezing occasionally.

If you can't be bothered to lie, you're telling your coworkers that you don't care. Showing that kind of disrespect will almost certainly earn you a drastic cut in hours and the closing shift on every major holiday.

2. Don't Be Obvious

You should be "sick" so infrequently that nobody even considers calling you on it. Your coworkers aren't stupid. If you call out every other Friday night, they're going to catch on. It's completely acceptable to call out once in a while when something really cool comes up, but you can't just ditch work every time you feel like going to the bar—that's weak.

Also, don't ask six different people to cover your shift on a certain night, and then call out sick when nobody can help you. If it's really important for you to have the night off, don't risk asking people to cover for you—just call in sick at the last minute. Trust me, it's better to have your coworkers *think* that you're faking sick than to *know* that you are.

3. Don't Exaggerate

When calling out sick, a simple and vague description of your alleged illness is sufficient. Don't trump up your fake sickness to absurdity to make your absence seem more justified—it's insulting. Unless you're already abusing the system and calling out every week, nobody will ask or expect you to elaborate. Why tip your hand with some unlikely affliction when a simple cold will do?

Believe it or not, on more than one occasion I've had an employee call in and claim they couldn't come in because they'd been "puking up blood all morning"—only to have them show up the next day in perfect health.

Now I've thrown up occasionally during my life, as have we all, but never have I found myself puking up blood, and certainly not "all morning." I'm no doctor, but I think if someone were to literally vomit blood continuously for a stretch of several hours, they would probably die.

If I was retching blood *28 Days Later*-style, I don't think I would bother calling work—I would just dial 911 and deal with my pissed-off coworkers later . . . if I survived.

4. Don't Be Rude

So long as your coworkers are using proper etiquette when they call in sick, it is extremely offhand to accuse them of lying even if you suspect they are. You don't want anyone calling your bluff the next time you have to invent some faux malady, do you?

As long as they're following the rules, show your fellow employees some courtesy and don't bust their chops.

5. Don't Waste Sick Days on Real Illness

It's fine to call out when you're on your deathbed, but don't call in every time you have the sniffles. If you call in every time you're legitimately sick, then your overall call-ins will be excessive when you combine them with all the times you've faked illness.

Nobody will blame you if you have to feign an ailment to use the Red Sox tickets you scored, but if you call out every time you have a little cold, too—well, that's just rude.

Play the game all you want, but when that real cold comes along, you have to suck it up and go to work.

RECOVERY

Depending on what store you work for and what day of the week it is, cleaning up at the end of the night can be either a chore or a freaking nightmare. It won't be at all unusual for you to spend several hours refolding shirts and putting a mountain of crap back where it goes.

Nightly recovery in the average store goes something like this:

1. Each employee is assigned a section of the store to recover.
2. Each employee quickly walks their section with a shopping cart, straightening the shelves and filling their cart with the out-of-place merchandise they find as they go.
3. When everyone is finished, each employee parks their full cart of random crap near the front of the store.
4. The random crap the employees found is combined with the random crap the pack rats have left at the registers all day.
5. All the employees chip in and spend the next ___ hour(s) putting all the returns back where they belong.

As daunting as this nightly horror can be, it isn't surprising that most employees will try to cut corners at clean-up time. The most common way to keep recovery time to an absolute minimum is by hiding a good portion of the random merchandise at the end of the night rather than hunting down where it goes. This short cut is known as "ditching."

Management generally frowns upon ditching, but since they want to go home at a decent hour, too, they often choose to turn a blind eye toward it. So long as the ditching isn't done openly and is kept to a minimum, managers will usually pretend not to notice.

That being said, you still need to follow these basic rules of conduct when ditching.

1. Only Ditch in Your Own Section

Each employee is ultimately responsible for the section they are assigned to clean, so they stand to be blamed for any obviously ditched items that a crabby manager might come across. Therefore ditching your returns in another employee's assigned area is strictly out of bounds.

The section you get assigned to clean at night is luck of the draw. You can't always get the best section for hiding things in. It's just the way it goes—you win some, you lose some.

Don't punish a coworker for being fortunate enough to score the aisle with the big clay pots or the laundry hampers.

2. Don't Ditch Anything That's Breakable, Sharp, or Contains Liquid

This should go without saying, but don't ditch any item that's going to tumble out of its hiding place, shattering and/or severing an artery when somebody stumbles upon it unwittingly. Nor should you ditch any item containing a liquid that can potentially leak and destroy whatever you hid it in.

Nobody should have to tell you that hiding a hacksaw, a

fishbowl, and a bottle of lamp oil inside a wicker basket on a shelf six feet off the floor is a bad idea.

Don't be an idiot.

3. Don't Ditch Items That Are Easily Recoverable

Don't ditch something if you know exactly where it goes and it's easy to get it there. Ditching should be reserved for the odds and ends that are tedious to find, not for anything you simply can't be bothered to put back.

A moderate amount of ditching is justified when your store is so understaffed that it's impossible to recover it the right way in a reasonable amount of time. But remember, the whole reason you have to put all this stuff back in the first place is because so many people in this world are too lazy to do it themselves. If you emulate that behavior, you're no better than the customers you're picking up after.

Refrain from laziness in ditching, lest you *become* one of the displacers you hate so much.

CHAPTER 11

Sales

Retailers are constantly exploring new ways to drive business in their stores. Increasing sales is a constant goal, be it through dazzling new products, competitive pricing, or clever marketing.

While retailers can control their product lines and advertising from the home office, they have to rely on their salespeople at the store level to further maximize profits. A well-trained salesperson can help drive a store's business if he or she is knowledgeable, has a helpful personality, and has a general talent for convincing people to buy things they don't want or need.

As a sales associate, there are four basic ways that you may be expected to harass each customer into putting more cash into your employer's pocket.

1. Up-Selling

Up-selling is when a salesperson tries to convince the customer to add options to the product they're buying, or to buy a more expensive (and presumably better quality) product altogether.

Talking consumers into an upgrade is always difficult, but some products are definitely easier to up-sell than others. While it's easy to point out what's special about a particular digital camera or computer, it's a lot trickier to tout the performance benefits of the "Cadillac of spatulas."

2. Add-On Selling
Add-on, or "suggestive" selling as it is sometimes called, is when a salesperson tries to sell the customer additional merchandise that is complementary to their core purchase.

For most consumers, the effective add-on selling technique of a salesperson is the only reason they have a pair of shoe trees or a can of Scotchguard collecting dust in a forgotten corner of their closet.

3. Selling Warranties and Service Plans
Some retailers offer extended warranties and/or service plans on some big-ticket items, such as electronics and computers, to give consumers a limited form of extended insurance on their purchases. Consumers won't volunteer to sign up for these costly benefits, so without the salespeople to push them, retailers are denied a big chunk of free money.

While paying out far less than they take in on service plans is an obvious plus for retailers, offering a warranty on a product also helps to lower the consumer's expectation as to how long it will last— otherwise, you have only the individual's perceived value of the item to guide them.

"Twelve hundred dollars is a lot of money, so this computer better last forever . . . and be virus-proof . . . and be able to withstand my rage when I beat on the keyboard after losing a bundle at the virtual blackjack table!"

4. Pushing Credit Cards
Many retailers now offer their own line of credit to consumers, and most who do will claim that much (if not most) of their profits come from the interest payments to their credit cards.

Strangely, credit cards are often the easiest thing for a salesperson or cashier to sell. Consumers seem all too willing to accept a one-time 10-percent discount on their current purchase in exchange for the "benefit" of paying 18 percent interest on all the future purchases they can't afford.

Depending on the disposition of the retailer you work for and/or your job title, you may not be expected to do any of these things. But the longer you work in retail the higher the odds are that you'll one day find yourself working for a store that still wastes money training its employees to do things they won't bother doing unless the manager is standing right next to them—so the information in this chapter is still good to know.

ROLE-PLAY: IT'S SO EASY
WHEN WE'RE PRETENDING

Selling things is difficult—especially when the product in question is expensive or seemingly unnecessary. Convincing customers to purchase things they wouldn't otherwise buy is a problem as old as retail itself. To teach you how to overcome this problem, your employer may use a technique called "role-play."

Role-playing is an exercise in which the teacher takes on the role of the customer to train the novice salespeople how to respond to the typical ways people will resist a sales pitch. If you're lucky, the retailer you work for will miss the point of role-playing entirely and create a training video of other people role-playing for you to watch rather than having you do the exercise in real life. Then you can simply watch some bad actors pretend to be customers and employees responding to each other in idyllic fashion. If you're unlucky, you'll have to suffer through the awkward ordeal of real life role-playing one-on-one with your manager or supervisor.

Either way, it's important to realize that the techniques you'll be taught in these role-playing sessions propagate the following false premise:

When a customer turns down a sales pitch, his objections represent honest concerns that can be overcome.

Allow me to illustrate why this premise is false by using a segment from a real instructional video I was once shown on how to sell shoe trees.

A customer and salesman stand on opposite sides
of a generic counter set against a black background.
A shoebox sits on the counter and the customer takes
out his wallet.

CUSTOMER: Okay, I like these shoes. I'll take them.

SALESMAN: Great! Do you have a set of cedar shoe trees for them?

CUSTOMER: Shoe trees?

The salesman produces a set of shoe trees from beneath the counter.

SALESMAN: Yes, you should always keep a set of cedar shoe trees in your dress shoes whenever you're not wearing them. It helps keep them in shape and will dramatically increase the life of the shoes.

CUSTOMER: Oh. Uh, no thanks, I'm not that tough on my shoes.

SALESMAN: Well, they'll not only increase the life and appearance of your shoes, but they'll also help to deodorize them with a fresh cedar smell.

CUSTOMER: Actually, I think I have a pair of plastic ones at home somewhere.

SALESMAN: Gee, you know, plastic shoe trees are actually bad for your shoes. The plastic repels the moisture back into the shoe leather. Cedar shoe trees absorb that moisture, allowing your shoes to dry properly.

CUSTOMER: Well, I won't be wearing them that much anyway.

SALESMAN: That's even more of a reason to use shoe trees. It's when shoes sit in the closet unused that they begin to flatten and lose their shape.

CUSTOMER: Uh . . .

SALESMAN: You know sir, we offer a thirty-day unconditional guarantee on all our products. Why don't you buy a pair of our quality cedar

shoe trees and try them out. If you're not
convinced that they'll keep your shoes looking
great, you can bring them back within thirty
days for a full refund.

CUSTOMER: All right, I'll get a pair.

SALESMAN: Great. You'll be glad you did.

End scene!

With the exception of the last two lines, let's pretend for the
sake of argument that this exchange could actually happen
between two human beings on the planet Earth as written. If I
were that customer, my inner thought process would go something like this:

CUSTOMER: Okay, I like these shoes. I'll take them.

SALESMAN: Great! Do you have a set of cedar shoe
trees for them?

CUSTOMER: Shoe trees?

*The salesman produces a set of shoe trees from
beneath the counter.*

SALESMAN: Yes, you should always keep a set of
cedar shoe trees in your dress shoes whenever
you're not wearing them. It helps keep them in
shape and will dramatically increase the life of
the shoes.

CUSTOMER: Oh. (*Damn, I really walked into that
one. I should have told him I already have a
pair.*) Uh, no thanks, I'm not that tough on my
shoes.

SALESMAN: Well, they'll not only increase the life and appearance of your shoes, but they'll also help to deodorize them with a fresh cedar smell.

CUSTOMER: *(Yeah, I'm pretty sure I just told you no. Who uses shoe trees anymore? I got a plastic pair for Christmas once and I never even took them out of the box.)* Actually, I think I have a pair of plastic ones at home somewhere.

SALESMAN: Gee, you know, plastic shoe trees are actually bad for your shoes. The plastic repels the moisture back into the shoe leather. Cedar shoe trees absorb that moisture, allowing your shoes to dry properly.

CUSTOMER: *(This guy just can't take a hint. Seriously, has anyone used shoe trees since FDR was president?)* Well, I won't be wearing them that much anyway.

SALESMAN: That's even more of a reason to use shoe trees. It's when shoes sit in the closet unused that they begin to flatten and lose their shape.

CUSTOMER: Uh . . . *(What is this guy, a robot? Give it up already!)*

SALESMAN: You know, sir, we offer a thirty-day unconditional guarantee on all our products. Why don't you buy a pair of our quality cedar shoe trees and try them out. If you're not convinced that they'll keep your shoes looking great, you can bring them back within thirty days for a full refund.

CUSTOMER: *LOOK, I DON'T WANT THEM, OKAY?!*
I WON'T USE THEM! I DON'T HAVE 25 BUCKS TO
THROW AWAY ON SHOE TREES! GET IT?!

SALESMAN: Okay, no problem. I'm just trying to
help. *(What a dick!)*

End scene!

When someone turns down a sales pitch with an excuse,
they're not voicing legitimate concerns—they're just being polite. It's human nature to want to spare people's feelings. Rather
than telling a salesperson how they really feel about the product
that's being pushed on them, most people will come up with a
nicer excuse.

Of course, that's what *most* people will do. A fair chunk of society is *not* polite and will tell you to screw off in no uncertain
terms when you try to sell them something. I've yet to participate
in a role-playing exercise that teaches you what to say when the
customer responds to your pitch by saying, *"I think you're full of
shit and nothing you say can convince me otherwise."*

Contrary to popular belief, the real reason for role-playing
isn't to teach you some magic selling technique, but is rather a
tool for conditioning you to ignore rejection. About 10 percent
of the general public is sufficiently weak-willed and/or wealthy
enough to cave in under repeated harassment and buy what
you're selling just to shut you up or avoid confrontation. The
problem is that you can't always see them coming, so the only
way to catch them is by badgering *everyone.*

Since most of us don't like to badger people, your employer
knows that the only way they can get you to do it is by convincing you through role-play that you're not hounding people at
all. If they can fool you into believing that the spiel they've
come up with can actually *educate* the customers into a sale,
you'll be far more likely to regurgitate it on cue. If they told you
the truth, you'd be self-conscious about the 90 percent of cus-

tomers who will be annoyed or openly angered by your efforts, and you wouldn't bother.

Unless you have a cool manager who thinks it's stupid, too, you can't really get out of doing role-playing exercises, so try to have fun with them—especially if *you* get the chance to play the role of the customer. Then you can respond to all the sales pitches the way a real customer would and watch the manager squirm when he or she is stumped for a response.

Here are some fun ways you can respond to your trainer's sales pitches if you get to play the customer during role-play:

Can I interest you in buying _____ with your purchase?

- "I'll buy it if you give me a discount."
- "I shop here all the time. Why don't you throw that in for free?"
- "You mean that isn't *included* with it? Well, forget the whole deal then."
- "Can I hold you personally responsible if it doesn't do what you say it will? What's your home phone number?"

TAKING THE BLAME

Occasionally your store won't make its sales figures for the week/year. For whatever reason, you just won't do the same amount of business you did the year before. It might be because your product line isn't as strong, or you're not running that same sale you did last year; it could be the weather, or it might just be bad luck. Regardless of the primary reason your store isn't doing business on any given week, you always have to remember one thing—it's your fault.

That's right, you heard me. Whenever your store doesn't make its sales figures, it's because *you* didn't work hard enough. Don't even think about blaming the shoddy new merchandise, or the ridiculously high prices, or the sloppy new packaging, or the poorly conceived sale, or the horrible merchandising strategy, or the phenomenally unrealistic goals—those are decisions that corporate made, and they don't make mistakes. They know what they're doing. They have nice suits and good attitudes, so if sales aren't happening it has to be because *you* dropped the ball—plain and simple.

You think a snowstorm, or a power outage, or low foot traffic in the mall is going to excuse your poor performance? Well, think again! Corporate can't control those things—and anything corporate can't control is *your* fault. In fact, anything corporate *can* control is still your fault. *Everything* is your fault!

The buck stops with you. Get used to it.

MAKE IT HAPPEN!

When sales seem destined to tank on any given week, management will usually address the sales associates with a pep talk that lays out the absurd amount of extra business that is needed over the weekend for the store to make its numbers. Your manager isn't going to offer any ideas on how that miracle can be accomplished, instead he or she will simply end the speech by clapping his or her hands together enthusiastically and saying, "Okay, let's make it happen!"

When a manager tells the staff to "make it happen," they are in effect acknowledging that there is no real plan or even realistic possibility for the store to make its sales goal. He or she is literally hoping the staff can somehow use sheer force of will to magically create enough business to compensate for the insurmountable shortfall in sales.

This may seem ludicrous, but you should remember that the corporate office is essentially asking your manager to do the same thing on a regular basis. When the products, pricing, sales events, and advertising aren't drawing enough business, the corporate office expects the store managers to "make it happen" and offset the deficit—no matter how big it is. So it's only natural for the manager to pass those unrealistic expectations on to the associates.

When the boss says "make it happen," that's your cue to start getting your excuses ready. Of course, those excuses will be unacceptable, but you'll have to say something when the time comes to explain yourself.

CHAPTER 12

Management

Whether you're interested in moving up the retail ladder or are just plain curious about how the inner circle of trust works in your store, this chapter will spell things out for you.

MY MANAGER IS AN IDIOT!

There's a very high level of probability that at least one of the managers in any store you end up working for will be an insufferable prick of monumental proportions. In fact, it's extremely rare to work for a store that doesn't have at least one douche bag on the management team. If it's not *the* manager, then it'll be the assistant manager, or one of the shift supervisors. There's always one. And if there isn't one, just wait a few months. Someone will quit or get transferred and be replaced with a real shithead—guaranteed.

In the grand scheme of things, retail management positions are relatively easy to obtain, so people who are looking for a little bit of power to abuse don't have to work too hard to get one. Therefore retail management is rife with unsavory characters.

This isn't to say that all managers are jerks—far from it. It's important to know the difference between a manager who's an idiot and one who is just doing his or her job. Most of the unpleasant or stupid things your managers do are simply what they get paid to do. They're no happier about them than you are.

For the most part, your managers are just following orders. In most retail chains, there are very few decisions that are actually made by management at the store level. Years of "progress" in the retail sector have reduced the responsibility of store management to one of mere administration. They don't manage the *store* so much as they manage the *employees*—making sure they follow the rules handed down by corporate. Everything else is fairly automatic. Corporate buyers decide what products the store carries. Computers keep track of the inventory, electronically reordering merchandise as it's sold. The home office sends out directives that dictate exactly how displays are to be set up and what sales will be run on what days.

Try to remember that the lot of the retail manager is a difficult one. In most ways your store manager is given no control over the way the store is run, but is expected to take all of the blame when things go wrong. Take this into consideration before you judge your managers too harshly.

On the other hand, if you really suspect your boss just likes being a dick/bitch for no good reason, you owe it to yourself to make him/her miserable every chance you get.

First Impressions

When I was first hired as the assistant manager of the educational gift store where I dealt with "misspelled T-shirt guy" and "binocular lady," I had no idea what the manager would be like. He seemed decent enough during the interview, but I'd been around the block enough to know that didn't mean anything. I've worked for plenty of bad managers and most of them *seemed* normal . . . at first.

I didn't have to wait long to find out what this guy would be like. By the end of my first day on the job, I knew our relationship would be tenuous at best.

For my first day, I was scheduled to work with the manager during the day shift. It was a small store, so there was only one other associate working with us. When I arrived, I introduced myself and she paged the manager over the intercom. When he came out to the sales floor, we shook hands and he brought me to his desk in the back corner of the stockroom to start me on my new-hire paperwork.

After I signed all the necessary forms and pretended to read the employee manual, the manager took me out to the registers to enter my name and password into the system. After doing that, he quickly brought me back to the stockroom to show me where everything was kept. The second the stockroom door closed behind us he turned to me and said, "Yech, if I had my way, I'd stay back here all day. I hate people."

As I said, I was no greenhorn at this stage in my retail career, so his attitude didn't really surprise me. There are plenty of curmudgeons in store management. What *did* surprise me was his willingness to admit it openly to his brand-new assistant on his first day on the job. He might as well have told me, *"Look, whenever the two of us are here together I'm going to hide in the back room and make you deal with all the riffraff on the sales floor, so get used to it."*

This by itself was a bad enough omen of things to come, but it was something that happened at the end of the shift that pretty much guaranteed this guy a spot on my permanent shit list. To do the story justice, let me provide a little set-up.

The store was located in an urban mall with two large multi-level garages that you had to pay a fee to park in—shoppers and employees alike. Since it was located in a downtown area, the garage was the only realistic option for parking anywhere near the mall. If you worked there, it was pretty much the only option.

The garage charged a variable rate, depending on how long you were parked there and whether you got your ticket validated. If you spent $10 in any store, they would stamp your ticket, and you would get a cheaper parking rate. Employees could purchase

a monthly electronic pass or buy individual coupons at a discounted rate. Most stores paid for their managers to have monthly
passes, so they could park for free. The passes cost $80 a month,
so it would have been nearly impossible to get full-time employees to work there otherwise. Luckily our store flipped the bill for
the managers' parking, so I was all set.

To use the electronic pass, you pulled up to the automatic
gate and waved your card in front of a sensor, causing the arm
to lift so you could drive in and park—same thing on the way
out. On my first day, however, I didn't yet have a pass, so I had
to push the button and take a ticket to get in like any shopper
would. I figured the manager would have a card ready for me
when I got there.

Fast-forward eight hours later.

The day went as smoothly as could be expected and was uneventful other than the ominous "I hate people" remark at the
beginning. At the end of my shift, the manager thanked me for
a good first day and let me go. I had my coat on and was all
ready to leave when it dawned on me that he had never given me
my parking pass.

"Oh," I said, "what do I do about parking?"

He stared at me in silence for a moment. "Oh, yeah, I forgot
all about that." He glanced at his watch with a concerned expression. "Are you parked in the garage?"

"Yes," I said.

"Well, there's a trailer in the underground service garage
where they give out the passes. You'll have to go down there and
get one. You should hurry, because I think they close soon. Just
tell them you work for us; they should have one waiting for you."

"Okay, where is it?"

He gave me directions, and as fast as I could, I made my way
from our store on the top floor down five levels and through a
labyrinth of hallways beneath the mall to finally find the service
garage and trailer he was talking about. It was the kind of trailer
construction site foremen use as an on-site office. The mall was
new and parts of it were still under construction, so they were

using this as a temporary garage office. The trailer was dark, but I knocked anyway.

No answer.

From behind me, a voice spoke. "They're closed." I turned around to see a mall security guard. He was a tall, thin kid of about nineteen. His faux–state trooper gear looked too big for him.

"Oh," I said. "Um, I work in the mall and I need a parking pass. Is there somewhere else I can get one?"

"I doubt it," he answered matter-of-factly. "You could try the customer service desk."

"All right, thanks," I said, disappointed, and headed to the customer service desk on the lower level of the mall.

When I got to the customer service kiosk, there were two middle-aged women standing behind it talking. There was nobody waiting, so I walked up to the counter and waited patiently for one of them to help me. To my annoyance, they spent another full minute talking before one of them finally rolled her eyes and broke away to ask, "Do you need something?"

"Yes, I work in the mall and I need to get a parking pass . . ."

"You have to go to the trailer in the service garage," she said in an annoyed tone, cutting me off.

Freakin' animosity generators. I hate them. "Yeah, I know, but they're closed," I retorted, dispensing with my usual customer-friendly tone.

"So, what do you want me to do about it?" she barked.

"Look, I just worked an eight-hour shift and my manager forgot to get my parking pass," I explained. "Isn't there some way I can get a temporary pass from the mall office or something? I don't want to pay twenty bucks just to come to work today."

She huffed at my misfortune. "Well, you'll have to take that up with your manager. The mall office won't do anything for you."

This was going nowhere and my anger was starting to give me tunnel vision, so I decided to give up. I pulled out my parking stub. "Fine, can you at least validate my ticket?"

"No," she responded snottily. "I can't stamp your ticket unless you spend ten dollars in the mall. Get your manager to stamp it for you."

I swear I blacked out for a minute. The next thing I knew, I was on the escalator headed back to my store. I was never arrested or kicked out of the mall, so I assume I didn't kill or shout obscenities at the customer-service ladies during that brief period of missing time. More than likely my abuse threshold was just tapped out and it triggered the automatic failsafe system in my brain, sending me away on autopilot for my own protection.

When I got back to the store, I headed into the back room to break the bad news to the manager.

"I missed them," I said with a sigh. "They closed at five o'clock. The lady at the customer service desk said there was nothing they could do."

He looked at me worriedly. "Really? Hmm. Okay, well I'll get you a pass tomorrow so it will be here for you the next time you work. Sorry about that."

I waited a moment for him to offer some solution to my present problem of getting out of the garage, but he didn't. "Um, okay, what do I do for today?"

He shrugged his shoulders. "I'm sorry, but there's nothing I can do," he said apologetically. "You'll have to pay for today."

Unbelievable. Not only did he forget to accommodate my parking needs, but he didn't seem particularly concerned about me having to pay for eight hours of garage time. I kept my cool though. It was my first day on the job after all. "All right, I guess it can't be helped," I said. "If I keep the receipt, will the company reimburse me for it?"

"I don't know," he said doubtfully. "You'd have to take that up with the district manager."

"Oh, okay, so you don't give a shit," I thought to myself. Then out loud I said, "Okay, I guess I'll take that up with her then." Trying not to show how perturbed I was, I headed out to the sales floor to leave again. "See you in a couple of days."

"Yup," he said nonchalantly.

On my way out, I stopped at the registers to get my ticket

stamped so I could at least get the validated rate. "Hi, again," I
said to the associate, rolling my eyes with a smile. "I just need
to get my parking ticket stamped."

The associate looked at me timidly. "Oh, um . . . I'm not supposed to stamp anyone's ticket unless they spend ten dollars."
Her eyes kept darting toward the stockroom door as if she was
nervous that the manager might burst out and catch this exchange at any moment. "You'll have to ask the manger," she said.

This seemed odd, but I figured she was just making sure not
to break any rules in front of the new assistant manager. "Okay,
no problem," I said, letting her off the hook. "I'll go check with
him."

Again, I went back to talk to the manager. "Hey, is it all right
if I stamp my parking ticket?"

He looked at me uncomfortably. "Oh, uh . . . how come?"

"So I can get the validated rate," I said. "I've been here for
eight hours."

What he said next floored me. "But a validation won't make
much of a difference. It would only save you a few dollars."

I just stared at him. It took every ounce of my energy to not
let my jaw drop and gape at him with obvious disgust. This asshole wasn't going to let me stamp my ticket because it would vi-
olate the letter of some petty mall rule. It was his fault that I
had to pay in the first place, and now he wouldn't even do me
the courtesy of stamping my ticket! I couldn't believe it. It was
just a stamp. It wasn't like the garage attendant could possibly
know that I didn't actually spend $10 in the mall. What was
with these parking Nazis?

Still, this was my first day at my new job. I couldn't exactly
have it out with my boss on day one. "Uh . . . yeah, but it would
at least save me something. Without a validation, it's going to
cost me twenty bucks."

"Well, maybe if you explain the situation to them in the
garage, they'll just let you go through," he said, obviously trying to tell me no without actually saying it.

"Yeah right, like the minimum-wage employee in the garage

is going to give a rat's ass about my problem," I thought to myself. *"I'm sure they give any random schlub in the tollbooths absolute power to arbitrate such predicaments."*

"Besides," he repeated sheepishly, "a validation won't save you much."

"It would at least save me something, you ass!" my inner voice screamed. I couldn't take it anymore. I couldn't reason with him, and I couldn't call him on his crap on my first day, so I was out of options.

"Okay," I said giving up. "I'll talk to the garage attendant."

"All right," he said, sounding relieved that I chose not to pursue it further. "Don't worry, I'll be sure to have the pass for you next time."

"Thanks," I said emptily and left.

Of course I didn't bother hassling the guy in the garage. He did a double take when he looked at my ticket. He was hesitant to scan it into his register. "Dude, you know this is going to cost you the maximum rate? Why didn't you get a validation?"

"My manager wouldn't give me one," I said dismally.

"You *work* here and your boss wouldn't stamp your ticket?" he asked, shocked as he processed my stub.

"Nope," I said with a defeated sigh. The digital readout displayed my fare. I handed him a twenty-dollar bill and got no change back.

"Wow, what a dick," he said sympathetically as the gate lifted.

"Tell me about it," I agreed and drove off.

Our relationship pretty much went downhill from there. When I quit a year and a half later, we weren't even on speaking terms. The fact that I was starting my own business in the same mall and stealing half of his employees on the way out probably had something to do with that. But hey, payback's a bitch.

I made it a rule that my employees had to validate parking tickets for anyone who asked, without question—no purchase necessary.

GETTING PROMOTED

As I said, obtaining a retail management position isn't difficult in the grand scheme of things, but that doesn't mean you don't have to make some kind of effort. You need to display competency in something to get promoted. You can't go from slacker to supervisor—not directly anyway.

Before you go through the trouble of doing a good job on a regular enough basis to merit your promotion, it's important to consider whether a management position is right for you. A lot of retail rookies look to enter management for the wrong reasons. There are many bad rationales for seeking out a management position in your store, but only two good ones.

The two good reasons are:

• To get paid more
• To run the register less

These are the only two real benefits of being a retail manager. Depending on where you work, you may not get paid *much* more or have to run the register *much* less than the average drone, but these two benefits are still universally true on some level in every retail job.

Suffice it to say that any other reason for seeking a promotion is a bad one, but for the sake of being thorough, I'll highlight some of the more common misconceptions that often lead people unwittingly into a retail management career they later regret.

I Won't Have to Interact with the Customers as Much

Because managers typically run the registers less, they may in fact interact with a smaller number of customers than the average employee. But what they avoid in volume is more than made up for in intensity. While you may have to cope with countless problem customers throughout the day, your managers have to handle all the unreasonable and irate customers that you don't get paid enough to deal with.

When you're a peon, you can always pawn off the real winners on a manager, but when you *are* the manager, there's nowhere to

hide. Your customer nightmares won't diminish when you become a manager—they'll increase tenfold.

The Management Experience
Will Look Good on My Résumé

Sorry to break this to you, but the stigma associated with common retail workers extends all the way up to management. Your
retail management experience will help you get other retail
management jobs, but that's about it. Nobody at the account-
ing firm is going to be impressed by the shift leader position you
held at Stop 'n Shop—it's just a fact of life.

Of course it's not fair, but it's true. Sadly, most people would
be more impressed to hear you spent six *months* interning in
the corporate *offices* of Target, than to hear that you spent six
years as the store manager *of* a Target.

It Could Lead to a Position
in the Corporate Office

No it couldn't. Look, if you work really hard for a couple of years
you can easily get promoted to the level of assistant manager. If
you work really hard as assistant manager for a few more years, a
promotional opportunity to store manager may open up. If all the
planets are aligned *and* the district manager doesn't hate you for
no good reason, you might even get that manager position. After
that, the best you could hope for is to become a district manager.
If you were extremely lucky, you might be able to accomplish that
after spending at least five years as a store manager.

Assuming you could do all of this in the most ideal time frame
possible (one decade), it's extremely unlikely that you would be
able to progress any further before you could no longer stomach
the place, or the company went bankrupt. So the best career path
you could hope for through management is to become quasi-
attached to the corporate office as a district manager in ten years.

If you really want to get into the corporate office, all you
have to do is go to college, get any random degree, and you're
in. Corporate doesn't hire people who work in their stores.
How would they know anything about retail?

Three Things

If you still want to get on the management team in your store, there are three things you need to do consistently as an employee for a period of about six months. If you exhibit the following behavior religiously, you should have no problem ~~tricking people into thinking~~ proving that you would be an asset to the management team.

1. Do your job

This one's a no-brainer. Nobody will promote you if you're a slacker. You need to do your job well and without having to be asked.

2. Pretend to care about sales

At the end of the night, always ask the manager on duty if the store reached its sales goal. Act excited when it has, and disappointed when it hasn't. The only thing that keeps your manager out of hot water is beating last year's sales figures, so he or she only wants people on the team who care about those numbers.

If you're uncomfortable acting in this underhanded and self-interested manner, keep in mind that all managers themselves only care about sales to the extent that it allows them to keep their jobs, or earn a bonus. Pretending to care about something out of self-interest is okay, so long as you do it to appeal to someone else's self-interest. The two wrongs cancel each other out.

3. Feign a good attitude

Your manager needs the supervisors under him or her to have the ability to put on a good show when the district manager or other corporate visitors stop by the store. The executives in the corporate office expect all of the managers at the store level to have unlimited wells of patience, optimism, and unquestioning subservience. In their minds, an ideal manager is one who loves serving the customers and making money for other people no matter how much they get defecated on in the process.

If you can't pretend to have a good attitude, then you have no future in retail management.

CONDUCTING INTERVIEWS: IT'S EASIER THAN YOU THINK

Once you've become a member of the management team, you will of course be expected to perform management duties. One of the more intimidating responsibilities a new manager has to perform is conducting interviews, but it's easier than you might think.

As we covered in chapter 3, you need to ask the person you're interviewing some stock questions to see if they can make up plausible answers on the spot without saying anything stupid. Assuming they don't give you any wrong answers, there are only a few other attributes you need to gauge in any interviewee.

Confidence

Your interviewee should be mildly nervous. It's normal to be a little bit fearful of botching the interview on some level, so if the person you're interviewing seems overly confident, there's something wrong. Anyone who goes into an interview for even the humblest job without a shred of self-doubt is either a con artist or so well-rounded that they pose a potential threat to your job. Either way, they should be rejected. The last thing you want to do is hire a thief . . . or even worse, your future replacement.

Appropriate Attire

"Appropriate" is a tricky term when it comes to interviewing for a retail job. If you work at Hot Topic or a record store you can get away with wearing just about anything. If you work at Nordstrom or Brooks Brothers, you need to dress very conservatively. For the most part, you'll have to use your own judgment when it comes to gauging whether your interviewee is dressed appropriately for the job he or she is applying for.

There are some things, however, that are a dead giveaway that your interviewee has put no effort into making a good impression on you. No matter which retailer you work for, a good candidate for employment should never be wearing:

Men
- A hoodie with the hood up
- A completely unbuttoned shirt with bare chest exposed
- A "wife-beater"
- Promotional clothing touting a brand of cigarette

Women
- Pants with a word across the ass
- A Hooters T-shirt
- "Daisy Dukes"

Men and Women
- Sweatpants
- Sunglasses
- Headphones

Social Adroitness

Never assume that the person you're interviewing is blessed with the same social graces you and I take for granted. You have to be observant and watch for any red flags that indicate your interviewee may not be adept when it comes to interacting with other human beings.

Does shaking hands seem like a foreign concept to the

interviewee—like they've seen it on TV before, but never actually done it? Do they avoid eye contact with you? Do they mumble? Are they drunk? These are all bad signs.

Remember, this person's job will be to help the customers, so if they can't even mimic basic human civilities in an interview they won't be much use to you on the sales floor.

SALES MEETINGS

Retail is all about sales, so naturally retailers will organize sales meetings for their store-level management once or twice a year. As a member of the management team, you may be expected to go to one of these meetings. Usually only the manager and assistant manager are required to attend. Lowly shift leaders and keyholders have to stay behind to man the store and miss out on all the coffee, donuts, and hackneyed corporate motivational jargon.

The sales meeting will take place in a hotel conference room somewhere central to your district of stores—which usually means you'll have an uncomfortable one- or two-hour carpool with your coworkers or counterparts from another store to look forward to. The meeting will take up the greater part of a day, and there's a good chance you'll end up sitting next to the smug jerk that runs the flagship store in the Wealthyville Galleria.

"How are the designer labels selling in your store? Oh, they don't send you the designer stuff? Pity."

Corporate might disseminate a modicum of useful information in the sales meeting, but mostly the purpose of this gathering is to get the store managers excited with clever presentations and inspirational speeches. The hope being that you'll leave so pumped full of sunshine and a false sense of control that you'll forget all about bad buying decisions, stupid policies, and socioeconomic realities, and embark on a magical crusade to increase sales in your store with nothing more than positive energy.

Corporate is good at mind games, so this usually works on some of the new managers for a while. But reality inevitably hits them in a week or so and they realize what a bunch of crazy crap it was.

THE DISTRICT MANAGER VISIT

The district manager is the next in line above store manager in the long chain of retail command. A DM can oversee any number of stores in a small geographic area and keeps all the managers under his or her supervision in line by conducting regular inspections of their stores.

The disposition of your district manager will fall somewhere between "tolerable superior" and "vile despot of unspeakable evil." Either way, the DM is a mouthpiece for the corporate office, so he or she is guaranteed to be a pain in the ass. By nature, there can be no such thing as a completely "cool" district manager.

While district managers are fond of dropping by your store unannounced any old time for a surprise ball-busting, the official DM inspection for which your store is "scored" is always a scheduled event. A bad inspection reflects as poorly on your DM as it does on you, so it behooves him or her to give you a fighting chance to get the store up to snuff.

The instinct of many rookie managers preparing for a DM inspection is to work extra hard cleaning the store to make it as close to perfect as possible. While this seems to make logical sense on the surface, it's actually the wrong approach to take. The best strategy when preparing for a visit is to make a moderate effort to clean the store, but leave one or two obvious problems alone for the DM to comment on.

Although counterintuitive, the reasoning for this is simple.

All district managers share one common philosophy—that no store should ever get 100 percent on an inspection. Your DM thinks there is always room for improvement, so he or she will never give you a perfect score or leave you without some problem to fix.

Therefore if you work too hard cleaning the store, the DM won't be able to find anything legitimately wrong, so he or she will be forced to pick out some petty, asinine thing to make you work on. Then you'll have to spend the next week cleaning ceiling vents or untangling all the phone cords. On the other hand, if you purposely leave a critical display undone, your DM will have something to immediately seize on. Then the only thing you'll have to fix is a display that you were going to have to set up anyway.

Remember, the harder you try to impress your superiors, the more busywork they'll punish you with.

ACTION PLANS: PUNISHMENT IN THE FORM OF CREATIVE WRITING

Speaking of punishments, one of your occasional duties as part of the management team may be contributing to the mandatory writing of "action plans" whenever your store misses its sales figures for the week.

As the name suggests, an action plan is a written plan detailing the course of action your management team will take to turn sales around. The corporate office will claim that forcing you to do this whenever you miss your numbers ensures you will address the problem in a concrete way, but in reality it's just a punishment meant to humiliate you and deter you from missing them again.

Your store could miss its goal due to any number of reasons beyond your control, so making you write a plan of action to prevent it from happening again is pointless. But of course corporate presupposes that whenever you fail to make your sales

figures, it's due to your *lack* of action, as opposed to some extenuating circumstance or dumb luck. It's just another way for
corporate to point the finger at you whenever sales flounder,
and reinforce that everything is your fault.

The real slap in the face is that nobody will even read the action plans that you write. Your DM doesn't have time to give it
more than a cursory glance to be sure that you did it, and corporate is only making you write it to punish you, so what's the
point? They just keep it on file so they have your written admis-
sion of incompetence handy to throw in your face if they ever
want to fire you.

Even the busiest stores drop their numbers once in a while, so
you'll probably end up writing a lot of action plans. It can be
tedious inventing actionable reasons for a drop in sales over and
over again, but don't worry. *The Retail Employee Handbook* is
here for you.

Just pad your next action plan with any of these handy pre-
fab statements, guaranteed to work in any retail environment.

- We will initiate additional role-playing exercises with our
  sales associates to ensure they are doing everything they
  can to take advantage of each customer and maximize
  every sale.
- We will review our training procedures to ensure that
  our employees are being given the tools they need to
  succeed.
- We will give our sales team a refresher course in selling
  techniques to be certain they are taking advantage of
  every opportunity.
- We will open a dialogue with the salespeople to find ways
  we can help them understand the importance of their individual goals.

As you can see, the trick to action plans is coming up with
different yet equally vague ways to say, "We'll kick the salespeople in the ass."

If you only miss your sales figures occasionally, you can probably get away with recycling these four statements over and over again by shuffling a few words around. If you drop your numbers fairly often, then I would recommend you invest in a thesaurus . . . and keep your résumé updated.

CHAPTER 13

The Corporate Office

After working in retail has eroded your soul for a few years, you might begin to view the customers as the root of all your problems. The truth of the matter is that it's your own corporate office that's to blame.

Ultimately, it's the corporation's attitude that the customer is always right that fosters the insane feeling of superiority and entitlement in the masses who abuse you routinely. It's the corporation's greedy desire to crush the small businesses in every community with their rock bottom prices that's to blame for your tiny paycheck. It's the corporation's manufactured need to be a ubiquitous retail giant that creates the micromanagement hell you burn in daily.

Unreasonable customers are just a symptom of the disease that big corporate retail is spreading. People abuse you because they know your hands are tied by a greedy, faceless entity that thinks a buck is more important than human dignity.

Okay, well, I guess the fact that so many people are evil jerks who are willing to take advantage of your tied hands is a problem in and of itself . . . but you get the picture.

PEOPLE WHO HAVE NEVER WORKED
AT THE STORE LEVEL

During your retail career, you'll often find yourself wondering why the people in the corporate office make so many nonsensical decisions that cause you grief. The answer is simple—most of them have never worked in a store before and have no practical retail experience. The few who have did it so long ago that they only remember what it was like in an idealized way.

So when the corporate office creates policies that are ridiculous or impossible to follow, it's because they don't know or care what you go through on a daily basis. They just want you to execute their ideas without question no matter how insane, ineffective, or unrealistic they are.

Idea people don't concern themselves with practicalities.

A Picture Is Worth 1,000 Lies

Before I worked for the manager who wouldn't validate my parking, I worked as the assistant manager of a different "educational" toy and gift store, called Learningsmith. At the time they were rapidly growing and opening new stores. During this expansion, the decision was made to redesign the look of the stores. They would remodel the most profitable stores first, and of course all the new stores would be built on the new design.

As it so happened, the first new-design store was opening in our district and not far from the home office, so the merchandisers decided to take this opportunity to showcase the new aesthetics. Rather than setting up mock displays in the home office like they usually did, they would set up the displays in the new store personally and take the pictures for the upcoming floorset change there.

Since stocking the shelves and setting up a new store for the first time is a lot of work, they asked all the stores in the district to each send some employees to help get the store ready. One of the shift supervisors and I were sent from our store. We met all the other employees at the new store early and started unloading boxes right away. It was hard work, but kind of fun. The store had a cool new look and we had plenty of customer-free time to stock the shelves to perfection.

After all the main shelves were mostly stocked, the merchandisers grabbed a few of the employees (myself included) and had us gather the specific products that were needed to set up the display tables on the floor. The merchandisers handed us product lists for each table and made sure to let us know that it was now 3:00 p.m. and they were leaving at 5:00 p.m., so we needed to be quick. The hypocritical attitude that us salaried employees at the store level who regularly work free overtime to get things done should hustle so that the salaried employees from the home office (who easily made double what we did) could leave at 5:00 p.m. sharp did not escape me . . . but this story isn't about that.

As I gathered the products on my lists, I was delighted to find that I and everyone else was coming up short on the number of each product required to build the displays properly. I was delighted because Learningsmith was very hard on their store managers when it came to setting displays. The planograms from corporate were to be followed to the letter without deviation for any reason and we were lambasted during store visits if they weren't. Of course, the problem wasn't that we were unwilling to set up the displays the way they wanted, but rather that we never had enough of the merchandise required to do so. Even though our product levels were completely out of our control, it was never an acceptable excuse, and we would still routinely lose points on DM inspections for not stocking the displays with merchandise we didn't have. So yes, the other employees and I were absolutely tickled when the merchandisers were faced with the same problem.

Confused, the merchandiser I was gathering stuff for asked, "Where are the rest of the Blue's Clues puzzles?"

"That's all there is," I said.

She looked at me blankly for a moment, then started poking through the empty boxes surrounding the table she was working on. "There has to be more than three," she said, annoyed. "I need twelve."

I snickered to myself at her absurdity. It was the kind of thing a customer would say. After another minute of searching in vain, she followed it up with another customerism.

"Did you check the back?" she asked.

Believe me, more than a few flippant responses popped into my head. Alas, there were a few bigwigs floating around the store at the time, so I did the prudent thing and gave her a straight answer. "There's nothing left in the stockroom. Everything is on the floor at this point."

Irritated, she rolled her eyes. "Fine, *I'll* go check," she sighed, and made a beeline for the stockroom. I couldn't believe how much she was acting like a customer. The irony was palpable. Obviously the sales floor was not an environment she was very familiar with on anything but a technical level. She could probably spout off the measurements and floor placement of any display by rote, but if I had told her the puzzles were in the back next to the "wall stretcher," I'm pretty sure she'd have gone looking for it.

The stockroom door was propped open and I could see the merchandiser I was working with talking to some other people from the office. Nearby, the shift supervisor from my store was looking on as well. "Hey, maybe this will make them realize what we go through *every* time we do a floor change," she said sarcastically.

"I doubt it," I laughed.

Not long after, the merchandisers came out and one of them made an announcement. "Can I have everyone's attention? Unfortunately, we're coming up short on a lot of merchandise for the floor set. However, we still need to take pictures today, so we're going to have to fake some of the displays for now, then fix them afterward."

The next part of the announcement left most of us stunned.

"Now obviously this wouldn't happen under normal circumstances. It's only because this is a new store and we couldn't get all the products here on time." She spoke as though she were talking to a room full of sixth graders rather than a group of retail veterans. "We want to make it clear that under *no* circumstances are you to *ever* do this in your own stores. This is just so we can take the pictures."

A cursory glance at the faces of all the store employees indicated that they were all thinking the exact same thing—these people are beyond hypocrites. One spunky manager working in the back of the store just couldn't let it slide without saying something. "It happens to us all the time," he said loud enough to be heard, but to no one in particular.

The merchandisers were obviously put off by the comment,

but pretended not to hear him and went back to work. They padded and propped up the merchandise on the displays with boxes and random products to make them look good from the front, and took photos. When they were done, they went back to the home office without a second thought on the matter and left us to fix the displays they had doctored up with assorted crap.

Weeks later our own store got the floor set packet from corporate that had the fake display pictures we had helped set up. Coincidentally, while I was putting together the very same display I worked on with the merchandiser in the new store, I found that we were also short on the number of puzzles the planogram called for.

I looked at the nice high stack of puzzles in the picture, knowing that only the three facing out on top were really Blue's Clues puzzles, while the other nine lying flat underneath were all Arthur puzzles that happened to be the same size. I imagined a DM in some faraway district pointing at that planogram and *tsk-tsk*ing a manager for not measuring up to a photograph that neither one of them had any way of knowing was a complete sham.

Then I thought about the manager who dared to passively mouth off to the merchandisers that day. I imagined him being abducted in the mall parking lot by some thugs in a purple van with the Learningsmith logo on the side, never to be seen again.

MICROMANAGEMENT: WE DON'T KNOW WHO OUR EMPLOYEES ARE!

How does a retail chain maintain control when it has hundreds of thousands, or even millions of employees? Micromanagement, that's how.

The bigwigs in the corporate office can't possibly know all of the store employees on a personal level, and therefore can't trust any of them. Consequently, every single thing you do has to be guided by ridiculously inefficient policies that are designed solely to prevent you from cutting corners or ripping off the company.

Here are two good examples of how micromanagement creates inefficiency.

9:00 a.m.

One of my first retail management jobs was working as the assistant manager of a chain shoe store in an old mall in Rhode Island. Sometime during my first couple of weeks on the job, the district manager called the store.

"Hey, Norm," he said conversationally, "who opened on Wednesday?"

"Um . . . I did," I replied.

"Then why the fuck didn't you open the register until nine-oh-six?!" he screamed. "You're supposed to be in the store at nine o'clock *sharp*!"

Taken off guard by his swearing and anger, I stammered out my response, "Um . . . I had to . . . er . . . go to the bank first . . ."

"Bullshit!" he barked. "Let me talk to Mark!"

Quickly I handed the phone to the manager and listened nervously as he calmed down the DM.

Here's the micromanagement stupidity that led up to my rebuke.

The mall opened at 9:30, so we were supposed to report to work at 9:00 to get the store ready. One of our opening duties was to go to the bank each morning and get the canceled slip from the previous night's deposit. We had to do this *every* morning without fail, so that if any manager decided to steal money from the deposit, he or she would be caught right away. The bank we used to make our nightly deposits was located in a separate building out near the edge of what was a very large mall parking lot. It was literally a five-minute walk from the mall entrance to the bank. Since the bank didn't open until 9:00 a.m., it made the most sense to stop there first thing when I pulled into the parking lot, grab the deposit slip, then drive closer to the mall, park, and go open up the store.

What I didn't know was that the computers in the home office regularly checked to see when the registers were turned on every morning in each store to make sure that their salaried managers were showing up on time. So it was also a policy that the register had to be opened up no later than 9:00 a.m. If a register opened late, it sent an automatic "late opening" message to the DM . . . who would then call and swear at you.

So in following the policy that was designed to deter the managers from stealing deposit money, I was inadvertently violating the policy that was designed to keep the managers from committing payroll fraud.

Although my manager convinced him that I wasn't really showing up late every morning, the DM still insisted that the register needed to be open by 9:00 every day. No exception would be made for us. Which meant that every day I would have to drive past the bank, park, go directly to the store, open the register, then lock up, go back outside, make the five-minute walk to the bank, grab the deposit slip, then walk back to the mall . . . and hope it's not really cold, hot, snowing, or raining.

Somehow the fact that all salaried managers were required to work fifty-five hours a week to earn our forty-hour salary never entered into the equation. Working for free is always okay, but opening the register six minutes late to be efficient is completely unacceptable.

Quantity Key
I once worked as a cashier in an arts-and-crafts supply store. They sold some fine art supplies, but mostly they sold supplies

for every craft imaginable. Popsicle sticks, yarn, beads, felt, Styrofoam balls, feathers, silk flowers, you name it.

One year the company had grown to the point where they decided to switch over to a perpetual inventory system. Basically this is a system where a computer tracks every item a store sells, then automatically reorders merchandise when product levels fall to a certain point.

Retailers like to claim that this is the most efficient way to handle inventory on a large scale, but it isn't. It's simply the most cost-effective way to handle it. Inventory is always best handled by experienced people capable of cognitive thinking. Computers only know what they're told, so they can't see or correct mistakes when given erroneous information—which you can bet will happen a lot when you've eliminated all your costly experienced people in favor of cheap apathetic labor . . . but I digress.

One day I reported for my shift and hopped on a register as usual. A lady came up with a basket full of little foam brushes. They were on sale for five cents each, so she wanted to take advantage and buy one hundred of them. Fair enough.

I began to ring them up by punching in 1-0-0, and then the "quantity" key, but when I did, it triggered a register error. Thinking I must have hit the wrong button, I tried it again but got the same annoying beep.

I called over to one of the supervisors at the nearby customer service desk, "Hey, Amanda, my quantity key won't work."

She let out a heavy sigh. "Yeah, I know. Hold on a second." She quickly finished what she was doing, then walked over to my counter with her keys, stuck them into the register and turned it to the manager function setting. "Try it now."

I rang it up again and this time it worked. "What is it, some kind of glitch?" I asked.

"Nope," she answered contemptuously. "From now on, the quantity button only works with a manager's key. If you need to do a quantity, you have to page a manager."

I finished up with the customer before I inquired further. "Why the hell did they do that? That's insane!"

With a look that suggested she was both bored and disgusted by the steady stream of idiocy that came from the home office, she said, "Now that we're on the perpetual inventory system, corporate wants to make sure that we aren't just using the quantity key to cut corners. They don't want the computer to order the wrong items."

We sold a ton of items in various colors. The most notorious of them was cross-stitching floss—the colored yarn you do those little hand-sewn pictures with. People would regularly come up to the register with fifty or more different colors. They each had a different SKU number, so they each had to be rung up separately—you couldn't just count them and ring them up as the same item. The thing is, customers also routinely bought large quantities of the exact same individual items, so the quantity key was something we legitimately used frequently.

We were already trained to know the difference, but now that the integrity of our inventory depended on us being accurate, corporate decided we couldn't be trusted to do the right thing. Taking away the quantity key (thus forcing us to ring in everything separately) was their micromanagement solution. The caveat that a supervisor could enable the quantity function for us if it was really needed was of little consolation because on a busy day, it could take them five minutes or more to answer a page. Which meant it was actually faster to hit the "enter" key two hundred times than it was to page a manager and have them use their key. Either way, the customer was going to have to wait for no good reason.

"What are we going to do when it gets busy?" I asked in disbelief.

"Get yelled at by pissed-off customers," she said dismally.

And indeed we did.

When a retailer isn't micromanaging to prevent internal theft or keep their computers from ordering the wrong stuff, they're doing it to maintain standards and conformity. Since they don't know about or trust in the skills and instincts of their store employees, they can't allow them to make any decisions on their own.

While most retail companies would profess that they encourage their store managers to "think outside the box" or "be innovative," this is rarely the case. What they really want is for you to implement their rules without question, and then take the blame when they don't work.

At Learningsmith, I once had an idea to make our sales floor more accessible to strollers by moving a single display to a different location. I asked the store manager if I could do it, and he told me I'd have to ask the DM. I asked the DM, and she said no. The displays had to be set up exactly as corporate wanted— end of story. So I gave up. If the district manager doesn't have the authority (or guts) to move a single table on the sales floor in one store for a trial period, then what's the point of going any further?

The best advice I can give you is to not bother coming up with ideas. It's a waste of time that will just make you bitter and frustrated. In retail management, creativity is encouraged, but not welcome. Corporate wants you to be innovative . . . just so long as your ideas don't cost money, or involve doing anything differently.

One of the more confusing elements of the corporate psyche is their thin grasp on the concept of employee incentives. The people in the home office fail to realize there is a fine line where an "incentive" turns into an "insult" and actually has the exact opposite effect.

"INCENTIVES"

A friend pointed me to a newspaper article recently about a well-known retail giant that has repeatedly been in the news for violating the basic rights of its employees. I don't want to get sued by this very powerful retail giant, so I'll just call them "Big-Store."

In the article, Big-Store was trying to make amends for its behavior by "reaching out" to its employees with a new incentive program. The program was purportedly multifaceted, but two specifics the article highlighted were these:

- Big-Store managers at 4,000 stores will meet with ten rank-and-file workers every week and extend an additional 10 percent discount on a single item during the holidays to all its employees, beyond the normal 10 percent employee discount.
- The program includes several new perks "as a way of saying thank you" to workers, like a special polo shirt after twenty years of service.

After reading it, I honestly couldn't decide which one was more comically insulting. If I didn't know better through experience, I would have thought the article was a parody.

Just picture it! On the first day of year number twenty-one working for Big-Store, you pull into the parking lot in your beat-up, rust-covered '91 Toyota Celica. You're not worried about the temporary tire you've been riding on for a week, because it's Christmas, and you can get an extra 10 percent off of the new tire you've had on layaway for six months. Hell, you've got a spring in your step. You've got twenty Big-Store years under your belt and you're livin' large on an annual salary of $27,000. You walk through the automatic doors and one of the shift supervisors hands you a dirty FedEx envelope from corporate. Excited, you rip it open to reveal a wrinkled Big-Store polo shirt that's two sizes too big! A single tear rolls down your cheek as you read the touching form letter that accompanies the shirt:

Dear Employee #834592750282834283-A,

It is with great appreciation that Big-Store presents you with this commemorative polo shirt for your twenty years of loyal service. We could easily go on and on about what we think of your two decades of dedication, but we think this magnanimous gift speaks for itself.

We hope to employ you for another twenty years!

Sincerely,

Big-Store

PS: There is no second polo shirt for forty years of service.

This is how out of touch and insane the people in retail corporate offices are. They might as well be giving their employees a punch in the face for Christmas and a kick in the groin after twenty years—it would probably have about the same effect on motivating the crew.

I was initially shocked to learn that Big-Store employees normally only get a 10 percent discount. At first I couldn't think of any retailer I'd worked for that offered less than 20 percent, but then I remembered that the convenience store I had once worked for offered no discount at all. Somehow that still seemed like less of an insult. I think I'd literally rather get nothing than 10 percent. I'd much rather my employer be up front about not giving a shit about me than make some pathetically half-assed attempt at pretending they do.

The Contest

During my stint at the shoe store with the 9:00 a.m. rule, there was a contest. One year corporate decided to sell backpacks during their annual back-to-school sale. This was a one-time purchase and corporate wanted to ensure a good sell-through of the product, so they came up with a contest to see what store could sell the most units. The store that sold the highest percentage of backpacks by sales volume would win.

The incentive for the DM to have the winning store in his or her district was a cash award of $500. The incentive for the manager of the winning store was a 22-inch color TV set. The incentive for employees to sell individual backpacks was fifty cents in commission for each unit sold. So far so good, right? Well, here's the kicker.

The contest had one rule. All employees had to *wear* a backpack at all times during the contest.

I shit you not. For an entire month, we had to wear a backpack around the store constantly. Setting up displays, waiting on customers, fitting shoes on people . . . *constantly*. Our DM made it quite clear that if he were to walk in on an employee who was not wearing a backpack, that employee would get a written warning. Mind you, we were required to wear suits and ties at this job, too, so you can imagine what complete dorks we looked like.

Mall passersby mocked us openly, or just looked at us like we were hopeless nerds who just couldn't be separated from our precious backpacks. Customers looked at us dubiously until we finally wrapped up the sale and told them about the backpack deal and contest. Then, they felt bad for us. I swear a good 80 percent of the backpacks we sold were bought out of sheer pity.

"Sure, I'll buy one to help you out. Geez, you couldn't pay me enough to humiliate myself like that."

The real horror of it all is that we won. Humiliating us *worked*. Our dinky little store sold the highest percentage of backpacks out of any store in the entire country. The DM got his $500 and the store manager got his TV set . . . and all it cost them was *our* dignity.

~~SPIES~~ SECRET SHOPPERS

Another tool Big Brother uses to keep tabs on his faceless employees are secret shoppers. Secret shoppers are stooges hired through a third party to shop at your store periodically and grade your performance. Afterward, a copy of the report is sent to the corporate office, and your DM . . . who then calls and swears at you.

Your store will be graded on every petty rule the home office ever came up with and the ending report will never take into account how busy or understaffed your store was at the time. No extenuating circumstance is acceptable. As far as corporate is concerned, there is never a legitimate excuse for not crossing each T and dotting every I—especially when that excuse involves blaming them.

At one of the shoe stores I managed, I once got a failing score from a secret shopper who happened to drop by during a freak rush. I was the only person in the store and was literally waiting on six customers simultaneously. Nowhere in the report did it

mention that I still managed to sell a pair of shoes to every one of those customers—each of whom was openly impressed and complimentary of my familiarity with the stock. The secret shopper was more concerned with the fact that I didn't offer to measure his feet or try to sell him shoe polish. Apparently my ability to effectively make a sale to half a dozen people at once wasn't important enough to be on the questionnaire.

The only way I could have gotten a passing score in that situation would have been to let five customers walk out while I spent a ton of time doing everything I was supposed to for the secret shopper—who of course ended up bringing his shoes back the next day to judge how I handled the return.

Some information contained on the report will also make you question whether the secret shopper actually visited your store at all. I was once described on a shopper report as being "over six feet tall with blond hair and glasses." Which is curious considering I'm barely 5'9", have very dark brown hair, and 20/20 vision.

How to Spot a Secret Shopper

Secret shoppers can look like anybody, and unfortunately, good ones are impossible to spot. You'll likely never see them coming.

On the other hand, *bad* secret shoppers have a number of tells. Keep an eye out for any of the following behavior in your customers.

- Constantly checking their watch.
- Taking notes.
- A look of surprise when you don't ask them to sign up for something, even though they should have no reason to know that you're supposed to.
- A look of disgust when they ask you where a product is and you simply tell them, rather than taking them to it by the hand.
- Using retail/company jargon they shouldn't be aware of (i.e., "Is this the only seasonal end-cap you have?" or, "Where are the soft-lines?" or, "Can you show me your holiday trim and botanicals?")

If any of your customers exhibit these odd behaviors, be on the safe side and pull out all the stops for them.

THE VP VISIT

Ah, the fabled visit of the vice president.

At some point during your retail career, you will be threatened with a store inspection by the vice president of the company. You'll be told of this impending executive honor weeks in advance, and will have to spend hours every day making sure your store is immaculate.

I've had this experience at every single retailer I've ever worked for, so I can tell you with absolute certainty that there is only about a 3 percent chance that the VP will actually show up. Everyone will bust their ass getting the store squeaky clean, show up in their Sunday best, then get a call around six o'clock to let you know the veep had too many martinis at lunch and can't make it.

I'm pretty sure the vice president of any retail corporation only makes his or her way out to the stores every five years or so. I think they just threaten all the stores with an annual visit to get them to clean really well at least once a year.

In fact, during my fifteen years in retail, only once out of a dozen or more times did the vice president actually grace us with his presence like he said he would. It was one of the more eye-opening experiences of my career.

The Vice President
In the second year of my employment for the "educational" gift store with the manager who wouldn't validate my parking, we were informed of an impending visit by the vice president and were told to make sure the store was up to snuff.

Even though the VP hardly ever shows up for these things, you can't ever *assume* that he won't, so we did our best to make everything pristine. Reportedly one of the sticking points of the VP was stockroom organization. As an incentive for the stores he planned on visiting, he offered a $100 prize to the store with the cleanest stockroom.

Being a self-motivated assistant manager with a flare for or-ganization, I took it upon myself to get the stockroom in order. I spent my entire eight-hour day shift before the visit cleaning the stockroom. The only thing I couldn't get to in time before the end of my shift were two bays of merchandise. The rest of the store was in good shape, so when the manager came in at 5:00 p.m., I let him know that the only thing left to do was to fix up those two sections in the stockroom. Provided he got that done, I thought we had as good a chance as any to win the $100.

The day of the visit, my shift started at 2:00 p.m. When I got there, the manager approached me nervously. "They're on their way," he said. "They'll be here in about thirty minutes."

"Oh, good," I lied. Secretly I had hoped to miss the visit en-tirely. "Did you finish up in the stockroom?"

A guilty look came to his face. "Not exactly. We ran out of time, so I just neatened up the stuff in front and hid the leftover junk behind it."

"I only left you two sections!" I chided. I spoke freely, because I had lost respect for him long ago—that, and I was honestly pissed. "Now I did all that work for nothing!"

His aversion to my disrespectful tone was evident on his face. "Calm down, it still looks good. It's not like he's going to get up on a ladder and dig through stuff. He won't even know we faked it."

"Great," I said flippantly. "So if we win the hundred bucks, I get the whole thing, right?"

"You're so fresh, Norman!" he said, exasperated, and walked away.

Beyond all odds, the DM actually arrived with the vice president and his entourage half an hour later. This was a first for me, so I really didn't know what to expect. I'd never seen a VP show up before.

Introductions went around, and for whatever reason the VP decided to pick on me first. "So, Norm, why don't you show me around your sections and tell me about the products," he said in a very businesslike way, challenging me to prove myself.

"Sure, let's start over here," I agreed confidently.

The store was split into categories and each manager took charge of a specific area, making sure it was stocked well and looked like the planogram.

I began talking about the products that sold best in our "spirituality" section. When I finished, he asked the DM, who was looking on nearby, "Hold it. Do the specs call for the mini bonsai trees to be displayed in the packaging like that?"

We had these mini bonsai tree kit things that came in one of those cardboard cases that was designed so that you could display the product right in it. The planogram didn't call for its use, but the box was actually very attractive, with an eye-catching graphic, so I decided to keep them in it. It was slightly different from the planogram, but it looked nice.

Before I had a chance to answer, the DM chimed in angrily, "No, they are definitely *not* supposed to be displayed like that."

"No," I agreed. "But the display box looks nice, so I made a judgment call. I think it makes the product pop. It's one of our top-ten selling items in this category."

"They're in the top ten in *every* store," the DM said dismissively, and shot me a nasty look.

"Well, the box does look nice," said the VP in a noncommittal way. He didn't seem to disagree with my assessment, but he also wasn't about to condone my violation of visual standards. After an awkward pause he continued, "Well, let's move on."

I continued on through my section, purposely glossing over the "magnet therapy" bay I was in charge of. The company had recently bought into a line of magnetic armbands, back braces, and innersoles with supposed holistic properties. The healing power of these magnet things was based on hearsay and vague "studies," and the customers just weren't buying into it. Most people saw it for what it was—the pseudo-scientific snake oil du jour.

"Whoa, slow down," he said abruptly. "What can you tell me about magnet therapy?"

"Oh," I said reluctantly. "Um . . . they're not selling well."

His brow furrowed. "We've invested a lot of money in this product, because we believe in it," he said seriously. "Are you doing the demo?"

"Demo?" I asked confused. I honestly had no idea what he was talking about.

"You're *supposed* to know what the demo is," squawked the DM.

She was like a big fat parrot on the VP's shoulder. I wanted to kick her in the stomach every time she spoke. If there was some kind of demo I was supposed to be doing for magnet therapy, this was the first I'd heard of it. The product just showed up in shipment one day with a brief product sheet explaining what it was. No "demo" was ever mentioned. She was just trying to make me look like a slacker to cover her own ass.

"No wonder they're not selling," said the VP, with a raised eyebrow. He grabbed a box of magnet therapy innersoles off the display and opened them up. "Here, let me show you." He took out the innersoles and put them and the empty box on a nearby shelf. "Stand with your feet apart and clasp your hands together in front of you to make one big fist." He did it himself to illustrate.

"Okay," I said, and obliged him.

"Now," he said, placing his hands on top of mine. "When I push down on your hands, try to resist."

"All right," I agreed.

He began pushing down on my hands and I resisted as best I could. His staging gave him better leverage, so he was able to push my hands down about a foot before stopping. He maintained eye contact and a sly grin the entire time, which I found extremely unsettling. I wasn't entirely sure that this wasn't just some macho bullshit to prove he was stronger than me.

"Good," he said, then took the set of innersoles off the shelf and put them on the floor. "Now stand on the innersoles and do the same thing."

I looked down at the black, vaguely foot-shaped inserts. "Um . . . okay," I said, and stood on the innersoles. I clasped my hands together and put them out in front of me again.

His eyes met mine once more. "Now this time I want you to *really* resist, okay?"

"All right," I said . . . even less sure about the macho bullshit thing.

This time he put his hands on mine and clearly made about half the effort he had previously to push my hands down. Of course, with the macho thing in my head, I was also trying twice as hard to resist. He forced my hands down only a few inches before stopping.

A big, excited grin came to his face. "See?" he said knowingly and with all seriousness. "The magnets actually make you stronger!"

Never in my entire life have I had to summon the willpower I did that day to stifle a laugh. I immediately diverted my gaze from the rest of the employees who had gathered around to watch for fear that I would catch a hint of a smile on one of their faces and lose it. This guy was a complete nut job.

Unfortunately the energy it took for me to stop myself from laughing left me without the capacity to feign any kind of appropriate response to his little carnival trick, so I just looked around blankly and mumbled some incoherent nothing like, "Oh" or "Hmm."

His face told me that my lack of enthusiasm was duly noted, and he abruptly changed the subject. He turned to the DM. "Okay, let's check out the stockroom."

"Sure," she said, and quickly accompanied him to the back of the store. She made sure to shoot me some daggers before leaving.

I was drained and annoyed, but glad to be done with it. I'd had enough corporate insanity for one day. I decided it would be prudent to keep to myself for the rest of the visit, helping the customers more than I would normally to look busy and put on a good show.

Not long after they went into the stockroom, the shift supervisor, Beth, came out from the back with a worried look on her face.

"What's wrong?" I asked, concerned. I was sure she was going to tell me the group was back there discussing how they should punish my insolence.

"The vice president decided to get up on a ladder and dig through stuff," she said queasily. "He just found all the random junk Wayne hid."

That made me feel better.

CHAPTER **14**

Loss Prevention

Every retail chain has a department in their corporate office called "loss prevention" that is in charge of enacting and enforcing policies designed to limit theft by vendors, customers, and employees.

As mentioned earlier, most policies that make no sense on the surface are born out of loss prevention—such as throwing away damaged merchandise. Since the retail giants have created such a logistical nightmare for themselves with their size, they then have to institute draconian, Nazi-esque rules lest their own customers and employees drive them into bankruptcy.

SHRINK

"Shrink" is the standard retail terminology used to define loss of inventory due to theft or error. As a whole, shrink costs the retail industry tens of billions of dollars annually.

Statistics on the subject vary, but employee theft is universally reported to be responsible for the highest percentage of retail shrinkage—usually estimated to be between 45 and 60 percent. Customers are generally blamed for between 20 and 35 percent, and the rest gets pawned off on administrative error and vendor theft.

While I don't doubt that employee theft is responsible for a significant amount of retail shrinkage, I have always doubted it is responsible for the majority. Since most theft perpetrated by customers goes unnoticed, unreported, and unpunished, it's only natural that any hard numbers on the matter will be far lower than the reality.

Theft perpetrated by employees, on the other hand, is far more accurately reported. Internal theft is more often noticed because the employees are easier to watch and catch. Employee theft is *always* documented, and while it's not always prosecuted, it's still standard practice for the home office to send their loss prevention goons to a store and browbeat a confession out of the guilty party to put on file.

The result of all this is a self-fulfilling prophecy. Since employee theft is already assumed to be the biggest problem, more attention is given to preventing it, and therefore more internal theft is discovered than any other kind. It only stands to reason that the highest percentage of stolen merchandise found hidden in bags will belong to employees when those are the only ones that get searched. If the customers were subjected to the same scrutiny the employees are, I guarantee those external theft numbers would skyrocket above the internal ones.

Not that any of this matters. The store employees are the only ones held accountable for shrink as a whole, no matter where it comes from. In that light, the employees are made responsible for 100 percent of theft anyway.

Everything is your fault, so it's a moot point.

Apathy

All the bag checks, security systems, and micromanagement in the world won't significantly reduce shrink numbers in the retail sector, because they treat the symptom rather than the disease. That disease is apathy.

Retail workers are underpaid, underappreciated, routinely abused, and have zero job security. How hard are they really going to work to make sure their nonentity overlord doesn't get ripped off? Why should they care?

Apathy is the real reason theft runs rampant among the aisles in the first place. Outside of their stock portfolio, nobody really cares if the category killer down the street succeeds or fails. Nobody cares if the local shopping center is half empty. When it goes under, another soulless retailer and megamall will pop up to take its place in a convenient location near you—they always do.

It's not just professional criminals and street thugs who are stealing from retailers—the vast majority of shoplifters are average people who see an easy opportunity to get something for nothing. Most people simply rationalize their bad behavior on some level to subdue their guilt.

When you remove the human face from a retailer, it becomes easier to justify taking advantage of them. Stealing from old Mr. Witherspoon's hardware store is much harder on the conscience than stealing from Home Depot.

"Hmm, they gave that CEO they fired $210 million, so I guess it's not going to break 'em if I steal this hammer."

SHOPLIFTING

Each year shoplifting costs the retail industry billions of dollars, but since customer theft is perceived as less of a problem than employee theft, it always gets less attention. While you and your coworkers will be subjected to everything short of an anal cavity search every day as a matter of routine, the customers can only be shown open suspicion if you have them caught on video every step of the way from the initial theft in your store to the pawn shop in another city.

The hoops that your employer will make you jump through before you can even confront a thief in your store are so pedantic that you'll rarely (if ever) be able to bring a shoplifter to justice. Here are the steps that most retailers require their employees to follow before ever confronting a shoplifter:

1. Visually witness the shoplifter concealing merchandise on their person.
2. Maintain constant visual contact with the shoplifter to make sure they don't ditch the item before confronting them.
3. Notify a second employee to call security or the police without losing sight of the shoplifter.
4. Confront the shoplifter, but do not accuse them of stealing.
5. Detain the shoplifter until the authorities arrive, but under no circumstances should you restrain him or her physically.
6. Never chase after a shoplifter.

If you can't follow all of these steps precisely and in order, then you will be instructed not to confront the shoplifter. Instead you'll be told that you should simply ask the shoplifter if they need any help in an attempt to make them uncomfortable. That way they're likely to leave without stealing anything else.

Although this protocol is a practical way to avoid lawsuits filed by falsely accused customers or prematurely accused shoplifters, it makes it impossible to catch the vast majority of thieves.

Let's break down the rules above.

1. Visually witness the shoplifter concealing merchandise on their person.

This in itself is hard to do, since all retailers routinely cut their store's payroll budgets down to a bare minimum to save money. Ironically, this "money-saving" tactic drastically diminishes floor coverage and severely limits the employees' ability to curtail shoplifting . . . which, as I mentioned, costs *billions* of dollars per year.

If you're the only employee watching a 10,000-square-foot area while simultaneously waiting on three customers, it's not very likely that you'll catch even a novice shoplifter shoving merchandise down their pants.

2. Maintain constant visual contact with the shoplifter to make sure they don't ditch the item before confronting them.
In the event that you get lucky and actually see a shoplifter stealing, it is highly unlikely that you will be able to maintain constant surveillance on that individual—especially when you're waiting on those three customers I mentioned.

Thieves purposely wait until it's busy, so you can't watch them carefully. They're not going to wait until you finish up with your customers to steal.

3. Notify a second employee to call security or the police without losing sight of the shoplifter.
Okay, you're waiting on three customers at once when your "spider sense" tingles and alerts you just in time to see a shoplifter shove something into his bag. By some miracle, the three customers you're waiting on all have telepathic powers and unlimited patience, so they immediately and silently bow out so you can shadow the thief.

Now how are you supposed to notify a second employee (who isn't in your 10,000-square-foot area) without losing sight of the shoplifter?

No, you don't have a communicator ring. That was the Super Friends—they're DC Comics. Spider-man is Marvel . . . aw, forget it.

4. Confront the shoplifter, but do not accuse them of stealing.
Okay, in your stupid screwed-up world where Spider-man has a communicator ring (lame), you summon . . . I don't know . . . Aquaman to call the authorities. I mean why not? It's a bastardized Marvel/DC hybrid world, right?

Anyway, now you're left with a fun paradox. How do you confront the shoplifter about his stealing without accusing him of it? Most retailers will suggest you say something like, "Can

I ring up those [insert stolen item here] for you?"—which is tan-tamount to the same thing, but I guess as long as you don't say any hot button words like "steal" or "thief" the lawyers won't have anything to bite on.

5. Detain the shoplifter until the authorities arrive, but under no circumstances should you restrain him or her physically.

Ah, yet another paradox. How do you detain someone without making physical contact? Not that I'm suggesting you *should* at-tempt to physically restrain a shoplifter—that's a horrible idea. But how else *could* you detain them? Playful banter?

Well, retailers always suggest you simply ask the shoplifter to wait for the authorities to arrive and sort things out.

Yeah, that'll work.

"Hey, I know I caught you stealing and you probably want to leave and stuff, but I was wondering if you wouldn't mind wait-ing until the police show up so they can arrest you. Is that cool? No? Hey, come back!"

6. Never chase after a shoplifter.

Unless you really are Spider-man, this goes without saying. Frankly, that whole apathy thing I mentioned earlier sort of takes care of this for the most part. I don't know anyone work-ing for a retail chain who would chase after a shoplifter even if they were told they had to.

Who's going to risk their life chasing after some random thief who may have a knife or a bunch of friends waiting for him in an alley? Sorry, but I'd be hard pressed to chase after a guy who stole something that belonged to me, let alone some-thing that belongs to the inhuman nonentity I work for. Hell, I wouldn't even wind myself for them.

Most of the time, when you suspect someone of shoplifting in your store, you won't be able to follow the protocol. When that happens, all you can do is unsubtly let the thief know you're on to him, so he'll become uncomfortable and leave without steal-ing anything else.

Since only the shoplifters who get caught are reported, the vast majority of shoplifting incidents go undocumented. In my more than fifteen years in the business, I never worked for a retailer that had any kind of reporting method for shoplifters that get away or merchandise that's found missing after the fact.

Of course, the corporate office would never allow such a reporting method on principle. If the employees were allowed to claim that any merchandise was stolen externally, then they could use it to cover up their own thievery!

And statistically speaking, most theft is perpetrated by employees, so of course they can't be trusted.

Auuugghghhhhh!!!!

TURNING IN YOUR FRIENDS
FOR FUN AND PROFIT

Since by nature it is impossible for the existence of any retail chain to be truly cared about on a human level, many retailers try to appeal to the self-interest of their individual employees by offering cash incentives to those who are willing to rat out any coworkers they might catch stealing.

A common poster hanging in stockrooms around the country is one that offers a reward of $500 plus 10 percent of the value of any recovered merchandise for calling a 1-800 number and reporting theft by a fellow employee.

Managers are generally exempt from this reward, so I've never been able to take advantage of it myself. If you ever have the opportunity, I can't stress enough how quickly you should drop the dime on your buddy if you catch him or her stealing. Five hundred bucks is more than most retail employees make in two weeks, and more than some make in a month!

Seriously, don't let guilt get in your way. I know it's easy to feel sorry for the scumbag who's fencing your store's merchandise out of the back of his van. He's a real human being. The corporate office is just a big greedy black cloud filled with numbers and rules, but you have to look out for numero uno my friend. You take that money and don't look back.

Oh, all right, if you feel *really* bad for the thief you could try blackmailing him for the $500 first, but it's a lot more work.

Of course, the 1-800 number is confidential, so if the thief pays you off, you could still theoretically turn him in. Then you've doubled up to $1,000! Hmm . . . on second thought, he might still assume it was you and try to get revenge . . . unless you're still Spider-man . . .

You know what, this is getting complicated. Just take the $500.

INVENTORY: PLEASE GOD, KILL ME

Most retailers conduct a physical audit of the merchandise in their stores once a year. Once again, since the employees can't be trusted retailers usually hire a third-party inventory service to count their stock for them. There is one inventory service in particular that is almost ubiquitously used in the retail industry. I won't name names . . . but if you work in retail, then you know who I'm talking about.

Once an inventory date is scheduled, you and all the other store employees will spend a week or two super-organizing the store and pre-counting all the merchandise that's in the stockroom or otherwise hidden from plain sight. The more work you do before the audit, the better off you'll be. Anything that is tedious or difficult to count should be pre-counted. If you want the audit to be accurate, you need to make things as easy as possible for the inventory service.

The reason you need to make things so easy is that the inventory service has a corporate office that is just as screwed up as yours is. In order to stay the number-one inventory service, they need to prove to retailers that they can be fast and accurate.

The problem is that their accuracy can't reasonably be judged because—hey, guess what—they're the ones doing the counting. If after the audit your store has a huge shrink percentage, your corporate office isn't going to assume that the inventory service screwed up, they're just going to assume that you and the other thieving employees are to blame. Because as we all know, internal theft accounts for the highest blah, blah, blah, blah.

Since speed is the only standard the inventory service can be reasonably judged by, that's all they focus on—*at all costs*. Inventory services ruthlessly hound their auditors into scanning barcodes and punching in SKU numbers as fast as possible, so accuracy isn't what's going to keep them out of hot water. A sloppy auditor who is fast will be left alone, while a meticulous auditor who is slow will get raked over the coals. I don't know about you, but if my boss was constantly on my ass to go faster, I wouldn't be too concerned with accuracy—especially if any mistake I made that wasn't glaringly obvious would never, ever be discovered anyway.

Not to mention the logistical realities of inventory service work make the hiring pool less than desirable. Not too many upstanding citizens are clamoring to have their balls busted at three a.m. in random retail locations throughout the state for $6.50 an hour. By no means do I want to stereotype the average inventory service auditor. I'm just saying that type of work tends to attract a lot of degenerates. I'm sure the good auditors who are just trying to make a buck aren't too thrilled about working alongside the occasional ex-convict or meth-head either.

What to Expect on Audit Night

Corporate isn't going to let you close for a day to conduct your inventory—no way. They're going to make you do it at night after the store closes, so prepare to be in the store until the wee hours of the morning

When the actual inventory night comes around, every available employee will be scheduled to help out. The inventory service supervisor will show up with a couple of auditors a few hours before closing to set up their computer equipment and begin keying your pre-counts into the system. The demeanor of the supervisor may or may not evoke your confidence in his or her abilities. The last inventory I participated in sent a guy who looked like Riff Raff from *The Rocky Horror Picture Show*, so be forewarned.

Between the time the supervisor shows up and the store closes, the rest of the auditing team that's been assigned to your store will straggle in. There will always be at least two auditors who don't show up, leaving the team short. It's the nature of the business. Those two missing auditors are probably the meth-head and ex-con anyway, so don't worry about it.

When the store is closed, the auditors will start counting their assigned sections. Primarily, your job during the night will be to facilitate the auditors by helping them count and finding SKU numbers for all the miscellaneous merchandise in your store that won't scan. When you can't find the correct SKU number, your job will be to find a product of similar value and have the auditor scan that instead. If you can't determine the SKU number *or* value of the product, your job will be to hide that product in the back room somewhere . . . and when I say "job" I mean "inclination."

If all goes smoothly the inventory could wrap up as early as midnight—but it won't, so just pray you're not the one who has to open in the morning. If you discover any errors or merchandise that was missed during the count after the fact, you have exactly zero days to report it and have it fixed. Sorry, once the inventory people leave the store, it's written in stone.

Once during an inventory at the educational gift store with the vice president who was a complete nut job, the auditors accidentally entered the wrong SKU number for a giant remote controlled telescope we sold for $6,000. We noted the mistake on the inventory report when it came in a week later and notified the home office.

They refused to fix it, saying the system just wasn't set up to correct errors that far after the fact. We just had to take the hit. So sad, too bad.

A month later they sent us another $6,000 telescope to replace the one the computer thought we didn't have.

When the inventory results come in, you'll get a list of all the products you're missing and your shrink percentage. Generally speaking, if that percentage is higher than 1.5 percent, you've got some explaining to do. If it's higher than 2.5 percent, there are going to be some draconian changes in your store. If it's higher than 3.5 percent, you should brush up your résumé.

CHAPTER 15

The Mall

If you work in retail, chances are you work in a mall. Even if you don't now, a lengthy retail career will inevitably lead you to one. This chapter has a few useful tidbits of information on malls not already covered in the other sections.

THE HIERARCHY OF STORES

In any mall there is an unspoken hierarchy of stores that more or less becomes understood with experience. Your store's ranking doesn't necessarily grant you any special privileges, but is a good measure of how you can expect to be treated by the mall management and other mall employees.

The above chart illustrates where different stores rank in the mall hierarchy, from top to bottom.

Mall management shows a proportionate amount of respect (or disrespect) to individual stores and their employees based on that store's perceived importance to the mall. Anchor stores are destination retailers that drive traffic, while kiosks come and go like the wind and are viewed as having little significance to the success of a shopping center.

Oddly, the way you are generally treated by other mall employees follows the exact same hierarchy, but for completely different reasons. Other mall employees judge a store and its workers by the type of customers it attracts. Stores on the upper echelons generally attract adults with money to spend, while the stores near the bottom tend to attract teenagers who do nothing but loiter and clog up the corridors.

I certainly don't want to portray this caste system as fair, I'm only pointing out that it exists. Of course, no employee should be judged by the reputation the store they work for suffers from, but it's human nature.

You should try not to perpetuate this hierarchy, but you also shouldn't be surprised when the Bloomingdale's sales associates don't pal around with the crew from Popeye's.

SECURITY

With shoplifting, violent crime, and global terrorism on the rise, security has become more important than ever in shopping centers across the country. So naturally your mall will hire a good mix of teenagers and senior citizens armed with the best walkie-talkies and golf carts money can buy to keep the peace.

Mall security will be ever vigilant in their constant watch for mall employees who park outside of their designated area. You can rest safe knowing that whenever your store closes a few minutes early, mall security will be there to report you. You can feel secure with the knowledge that whenever a customer spills a soft drink in the common area, a security guard will be there to stand over it until a custodian arrives to clean it up.

The one thing mall security doesn't do is catch shoplifters. Contrary to popular belief, that's not really their thing. Like you, mall security isn't allowed to accuse people of anything or physically detain anyone. Heck, in most malls they're not even allowed to enter the stores, so their jurisdiction is often restricted to areas where theft doesn't even occur. The mall management is just as afraid of a lawsuit as your corporate office, so when you have a real security problem in your mall, calling mall security is the last thing you should do.

If you want to break up the group of thirty teenagers blocking the entrance to your store, call mall security. If you have a real situation that requires tangible authority and action, call the police.

There's nothing mall security can do for you that any big guy who already works in your store can't.

Master of His Domain
In the mall where one of the shoe stores I managed was located, we had a freestanding sign that we put out in front of the store each morning. The mall allowed us to do this, but the rule was that it couldn't be placed more than two floor tiles beyond the store entrance.

During their morning rounds, the mall security guards would check to see if anyone was violating the two-tile rule. Since most employees would toss their sign out without much thought, the security guards would walk the mall each morning and push offending signs back a few inches as a matter of routine.

This is all well and good, but I began to notice that the mall security guard who walked our level would nudge my sign back a few inches with his foot every single morning, whether it was over the two-tile limit or not. It really started to bug me, so one morning I decided to thwart his efforts by butting my sign right up against the rubber strip where my carpet began and the mall tiles ended so that it couldn't be pushed back anymore without removing it from the tiles entirely.

Little did I realize the joy I was about to stumble upon. That morning, when the security guard stopped at my sign and found he couldn't nudge it backward anymore, he tapped it a few inches sideways instead, then moved on. I was dumbfounded.

Convinced that I must have just thrown him off his game with the sudden change to his routine, I tried it again the next day. I was sure that this time he would leave it alone, but sure enough he did the same thing. He kicked it a few inches sideways with his foot, as if it wasn't centered in the doorway enough or something, then moved on.

This was too good to be true.

For the next few weeks, whenever I worked the opening shift I varied the position of the sign just to see what he would do to it. Some days I would make it crooked, some days I would place one of the feet on the rubber strip so it tilted a little, some days I would center it perfectly—and each day he moved it. If it was crooked, he straightened it. If it was tilting, he leveled it. If it was perfectly centered, he *un*-centered it! No matter what I did with the sign, he moved it. His ability to create useless busy-work for himself in an effort to display his administrative authority over objects in the mall common area seemingly knew no bounds. It was awesome! Messing with him became part of my morning routine and brightened my day.

Alas, all good things must come to an end. One day I took the game too far and put the sign completely on the carpet. I should have known that would be too much. That morning he stopped short and just looked at the sign blankly. After a moment he looked at me standing behind the register and caught me watching him—I couldn't divert my gaze quickly enough.

He walked away uncomfortably with the angry/hurt look of someone who discovers he's been the secret object of someone's ridicule and the game was over forever. I even threw him a bone the next day and put the sign slightly over the second tile, but he just walked past without even looking at it. He never touched my sign again.

It serves me right, I suppose. I got greedy.

PARKING

At every mall, the employees are required to park in designated areas that are as far away from the mall entrance as humanly possible. The reason for this is simple. The mall wants to reserve the best parking spaces for its patrons.

In most respects, this is a reasonable demand. If the employees were allowed to park wherever they pleased, the front three spaces of every row in the lot would be filled before the mall even opened. Where I believe this rule crosses the line is that employees aren't simply forbidden to take the best spots, they're forced to use the absolute *worst* parking spots under the threat of having their cars towed.

Argue the effect that limited mall parking has on consumer

habits and psychology all you want, but that doesn't change the fact that the customers have no way of knowing where the employee vehicles are. No one in the history of the world has ever pulled into a jam-packed mall parking lot and said, *"Damn it, look how many of these cars up front belong to employees! This mall obviously doesn't care about my convenience! I'm leaving!"*

Sure, it's a good bet that any rust-covered beater with a broken side-view mirror and a bumper held on with rope *probably* belongs to a retail employee, but you couldn't know that for certain. Once the lot's full, the lot's full. What does it matter where the employees are parked? Nobody will know the difference.

The decent thing to do would be to let the opening employees park anywhere except for the first four or five spaces of any row. That way they don't have to walk the span of the entire lot every day, and the customers who show up as soon as the mall opens can see that the mall workers didn't snag up all the best spots. After that, the lot is just a jumble of anonymous cars anyway, so the nicety doesn't really cost anything.

Being decent to retail employees has never been in vogue, however, so the mall will make you park in a detached lot at least 500 yards from the closest entrance, or the top level of the garage.

Ironically, the mall has difficulty enforcing the employee parking rule for the very same reason it shouldn't be an issue in the first place—they have no way of identifying employee cars in a lot of thousands. This being the case, the mall management requires each store to periodically supply them with a list of employee vehicles, complete with make, model, and license plate number. Armed with this information, mall security will cruise the regular lot to make sure that no employee vehicles are parked "illegally" . . . while the cars parked in the isolated and unwatched employee lot get broken into and vandalized.

Realistically, there are going to be days that you're running late and will be tempted to park closer to the entrance than you're supposed to. Since the mall will have your car towed if they discover it, you need to safeguard yourself.

If you follow these simple guidelines, you should be able to occasionally break the parking rules undetected.

1. Never talk to mall security.
The last thing you want is for mall security to become familiar with your face. Most employees get caught parking out of bounds when a security guard sees them getting out of their car and recognizes them.

If you're an attractive woman, this is going to be nearly impossible for you. The security guards will invent reasons to talk to you and probably leer at you from the mall on a daily basis without you even knowing it.

Sorry, that's the price of beauty.

2. When parking illegally, choose an inconspicuous spot.
If possible, park next to a large truck or van. If there's a parking garage, try to get a space behind a concrete support column. Out of sight, out of mind.

3. Give the mall a false description of your vehicle.
You drive a blue Ford Taurus and your registration is any random string of numbers and letters that fits the pattern of your state's plate sequence—unless you really do drive a blue Ford Taurus, in which case you drive a red Honda Civic.

You might be tempted to use the real plate number of someone you dislike, but I'd advise against it. As sweet as it would be to have your arch nemesis's car towed on his next trip to the mall, the paper trail will lead right back to you and you'll be in hot water. It's best to just pull a number out of thin air.

Holiday Parking

During the Christmas season, the employee parking rules get even worse. Most shopping centers will actually make their employees park in a temporary off-site lot a mile or so away from the mall and have them shuttled in. You'll have to arrive at the lot before dawn each day to compensate for both the mall's extended holiday hours *and* the additional time it takes to wait in the cold for a bus.

Yes, you haven't lived until you've had to park in a muddy unpaved lot in the middle of nowhere to wait in the cold for a beatup, overcrowded shuttle bus that eventually takes you and the other cranky retail employees to the mall you drove past twenty minutes earlier.

CHAPTER 16

Christmas

Ihate to break this to you, but the holidays will no longer be a magical or warm experience for you. No matter how near and dear you hold Christmas in your heart, your job as a retail employee places you at the epicenter of the unstoppable whirlwind of crass commercialization that the holidays have become. Put simply, you will be forced to participate in everything that is wrong with Christmas.

From now on, you will look bitterly upon the sentiments "peace on earth" and "good will to men" as empty and disingenuous catchphrases used only to sell greeting cards. The sound of holiday music you once found joyous will now make you want to bludgeon Bing Crosby to death with a Yule log. From this point forward, "Holiday Cheer" is just the name of a Yankee Candle.

The season of giving is dead to you now.

"HAPPY HOLIDAYS"

While retailers contend they use the phrase "Happy Holidays" as a harmless alternative to avoid offending their non-Christian patrons, many consumers see banning the utterance of "Merry Christmas" as an intentional ploy to marginalize the religious significance of the holiday. Even among consumers who see no such conspiracy, there are those who are simply angered by what they see as an unending and unnecessary trend toward political correctness in all aspects of life.

Each year, media stories stir up national attention to this issue. Religious groups will publicly boycott retailers they accuse of trying to "take Christ out of Christmas." Humorists will ritually lampoon the topic with parodies of cashiers offering ludicrously over-sensitive holiday greetings. News outlets will conduct polls and man-on-the-street interviews.

Despite the attention the media gives to this topic every single holiday season, there are two important points that always seem to be left out of the discussion.

1. The retail, food service, and hospitality industries have been using the phrase "Happy Holidays" in place of "Merry Christmas" for at least the last twenty years.
2. Nobody gives a shit.

How long are the vocal minorities going to pretend this non-issue we've been living with for the last two decades is some totally new and abhorrent thing? Is there no end to the petty things people will bitch about? Are people really afraid that the counter help at Target is going to singlehandedly wipe Christianity off the map with their generic holiday greetings? Is being thoughtful and considerate of the beliefs of others really that much of a chore?

Thanks to the complainers, retail workers aren't even safe saying "Happy Holidays" anymore. What was once an all-purpose, non-offending salutation is now bait for some fundamentalist nut's diatribe about how far America has gone down the toilet.

There's just no pleasing some people, so my advice to you is to say, "Have a nice day/night," during the holidays like you do the rest of the year. Sure it's cold and soulless, but it's the only way to make sure you don't offend the people who are offended by the fact that society is obsessed with not offending people.

The more crap you can avoid during Christmas, the better.

THE 120 DAYS OF CHRISTMAS

For most retailers, Christmas begins in late September with the beginning of holiday merchandise shipments, and ends in mid to late January when consumers have finally spent all of their gift cards, returned or exchanged their unwanted gifts, and picked through the last of the holiday clearance.

This is just the average, of course. Depending on where you work, you could begin receiving Christmas-themed merchandise even earlier than September. The arts-and-crafts supply store I used to work for annually received and displayed their first batch of Christmas-themed merchandise in mid July . . . that's right, do the math. That meant there were only five months out of the year that were Christmas-free. We were fresh out of holiday spirit by August.

Can you imagine focusing that much attention on any other holiday? The other three über-commercialized holidays—Valentine's Day, Easter, and Halloween—don't take up as much time combined. We've reached the point where Halloween has to *share* time with Christmas—rubber masks and fake vampire teeth in one aisle, tinsel and colored lights in the next. It's insane!

As omnipresent as Christmas will be during half of every year you work in retail, don't let it get you down too much. Let it strengthen your resolve to celebrate the holidays in healthy and meaningful ways. Let it remind you that Christmas doesn't come from a store. Let it remind you that maybe Christmas . . . perhaps . . . means a little bit more.

I find it crushingly sad and ironic that although *How the Grinch Stole Christmas* has been read annually to every child since 1957, it has been entirely unsuccessful in proliferating its core message. Throw in the fact that it's also been an astronomical commercial success if you want to add to that irony, but I think I've made my point.

CHRISTMAS HELP

Retail work is easy to come by any time of the year, but at no time is it easier to get a job behind a register than at Christmas. Retail's already low hiring standards have to be thrown right out the window during the holidays. The sheer amount of temporary help required to handle the increased holiday traffic simply does not allow for anything but the most basic screening process . . . which leads to your store hiring a bunch of last-minute slobs, thieves, and crazy people every November.

Not all Christmas help is bad. A lot of people break into their retail careers during the holidays. Any Christmas helper who turns out *not* to be a complete loser usually gets honored with an invitation to become a regular wage slave after January. Anybody who still wants to stay after handling an entire holiday season without any previous retail experience is definitely a ~~sadomasochist~~ keeper.

As a manager, it's best to hire about twice as many holiday helpers as you actually need, since most of them will quit or have to be fired way before Christmas. Likewise, twice as many Christmas helpers as needed should be scheduled to every shift during the holidays. Christmas help is notoriously naïve about the workplace, so they generally have no idea that their work schedule is anything more than a suggestion. It's best to hedge your bets so you're not left shorthanded by a bunch of temps who all simultaneously "forgot they were working."

Unfortunately, hiring a bunch of apathetic, socially inept automatons each Christmas is a necessary evil in the retail industry. As if retail workers didn't suffer enough from the negative stereotypes perpetuated by curmudgeons and animosity generators, the incompetent holiday help will fuel them even more.

Christmas Hinderer
One Christmas at the arts-and-crafts supply store I used to be a cashier for, they hired this kid, whom I will call "Vinnie," as one of the holiday helpers.

I think my first inkling that Vinnie wasn't cut out for this line of work was when we were running some stock together one day and he worriedly asked me, "Are you ever afraid that people will think you're a fag because you work here?"

"No," I said flatly. "Why would I care if some idiot thought that?"

This stumped him of course, because in his world that was the worst thing somebody could think about you. In my world, the worst thing somebody can think about you is that you're the kind of moron who thinks working in a craft store might turn you gay.

In the following days of his short employment with the company, Vinnie would commit many other faux pas.

On his first closing night, he punched out, put on his coat, and headed for the door the moment we locked up. The assistant manager had to break the news to him that working "five to close" wasn't meant literally. There were no elves coming to clean the place up for us—we had to do it ourselves.

Another night he threw two full cases of artificial wreaths into the cardboard compactor. Apparently the weight of the boxes wasn't enough to tip him off that they weren't empty. I'm pretty sure the retail cost of those wreaths far exceeded what they paid him during his short stay.

When he wasn't screwing something up, he was spouting some ignorant trash like, "I shouldn't have to sweep the floor! That's women's work!" Yeah, he was a big hit with our 90-percent female staff.

The best and final incident I can recall before Vinnie simply stopped showing up was a real treasure.

One day we got a huge shipment of around fifty cases of Christmas wrapping paper. The paper came in tall boxes that each contained twenty-four tubes. The cases were designed so that you could just cut the top eight inches off and display the rolls on the floor right in the box. After we had displayed one in every possible location, we still had a bunch left over. It was about that time that Vinnie came in for his shift . . . late, as usual.

"It's about time you showed up," the assistant manager complained. "I've got a job for you after you punch in."

Vinnie punched in and dragged his feet out to the seasonal aisle where we had the last fifteen or so cases of unopened wrapping paper scattered about. "What do you want me to do?"

The assistant manager gestured to the cases of wrapping paper. "There's no more room to display any of this wrapping paper, so I want you to lay them down flat and form a pyramid out of them at the end of the artificial tree display so they look nice."

He looked around at the cases dauntingly. "Who's going to help me?"

"Nobody," huffed the manager. "We've been doing this all day. It shouldn't take you more than ten minutes."

Looking pissed, Vinnie begrudgingly went to work. The assistant went on to do other things and I went on break.

After finishing my fifteen-minute break, I came back out onto the sales floor just in time to witness one of the most comical displays of real-life stupidity I have ever seen. As I approached the seasonal aisle, I heard the shocked voice of the assistant manager say, "What the hell are you doing?"

When I actually got there, Vinnie was sitting on the floor next to a big haphazard pile of loose Christmas wrapping paper tubes. The assistant manager was at the opposite end of the aisle staring at the mess in disbelief. Vinnie was red as a beet with frustration. "I'm trying to stack them in a pyramid like you told me, but they keep rolling away!"

Defying all logic, Vinnie had misinterpreted the assignment to stack the *cases* of wrapping paper, and had spent the last fifteen minutes opening the cases and trying to build a pyramid out of the *individual rolls*.

"Not the rolls, you idiot," the manager roared. "The cases! You were supposed to stack the cases!"

"Well, I didn't know," Vinnie retorted defensively.

Exasperated, the manager banished him. "Just go work on returns. I'll do this myself."

Vinnie stormed off, embarrassed, and I helped the assistant manager clean up the mess. He just shook his head as the two of us shoved the tubes back into the cases Vinnie had emptied. "Unbelievable," he said miserably. "Un-be-freakin'-lievable!"

TOYS WORTH TRAMPLING FOR

Every Christmas season there's some new toy or electronic gizmo that parents are clamoring to get for their kids. Over the years, there's been Cabbage Patch Kids, and Beanie Babies, and Tickle Me Elmo, and Razor Scooters, and Xbox 360—there's always some plaything that's in short supply and high demand that causes riots and utter chaos for the retailers who sell them.

Despite the fact that kids are never enamored with any toy or gadget for more than a few weeks, nobody ever seems to learn. For some reason, nobody remembers that the Furby they wrestled some soccer mom for years ago is now a forgotten piece of trash at the bottom of their kid's toy box. It just doesn't occur to some people that killing a guy to get a Playstation 3 might not be worth it in the long run.

It was Dostoevsky who said, "The degree of civilization in a society can be seen by entering its prisons." Sadly, you don't have to go that far. All you have to do is enter Wal-Mart on the day after Thanksgiving to see how completely batshit-crazy our society is.

You'll witness firsthand how damaged our nation's collective priorities are after you've worked your first "toy riot"—especially if said toy is unveiled on the day after Thanksgiving, or "Black Friday" as it's known in the industry. If that's poised to happen, you'd better stock up on pepper spray and trauma counseling, because you're going to need plenty of both.

There's not much I can do to prepare you for a "toy riot." I could warn you against working anywhere toys or electronics are sold, but that's not very realistic. All I can tell you is that if the experience doesn't kill you, it will make you stronger.

. . . and incurably cynical about human nature.

THAT GOES WITHOUT SAYING. COOPER, DID YOU TEST OUT THE EQUIPMENT FOR THE EARLY MORNING SALES EVENTS?

IT'S ALL SET. THE RIOT SHIELDS ARE PRETTY BANGED UP FROM LAST YEAR, BUT THEY'RE DEFINITELY STILL FUNCTIONAL.

OKAY, IT SOUNDS LIKE WE'RE READY. LET'S JUST REMIND ALL THE EMPLOYEES WHAT A FUN WEEKEND IT'S GOING TO BE!

11/20

4 DAYS BEFORE

BLACK FRIDAY

ONLY 4 MORE SHOPPING DAYS UNTIL CHAOS!!!

WHY DO YOU AUTOMATICALLY ASSUME IT WAS ME?

WHY WOULDN'T I?

11/21

3 DAYS BEFORE

BLACK FRIDAY

WHAT'S THE MATTER, COOPER? DID STUART SHOOT DOWN YOUR INSANE THEFT-CONTROL PLAN FOR THIS WEEKEND?

YES! APPARENTLY, BEANBAG GUNS AREN'T IN KEEPING WITH THE SPIRIT OF THE HOLIDAYS. GEEZ, EVERYTHING IS SO P.C. NOWADAYS!

OFFICE

ALMOST LETHAL

11/22

2 DAYS BEFORE

BLACK FRIDAY

ENJOY YOUR DAY OF FREEDOM, EVERYONE. JUST REMEMBER WE OPEN AT 6:00 AM ON FRIDAY, SO GET HERE BRIGHT AND EARLY.

DON'T WORRY. THE ANNUAL "NO-HOLDS-BARRED DEATH MATCH FOR THE LAST DVD PLAYER ON SALE" IS THE ONLY THING I LOOK FORWARD TO AT CHRISTMASTIME.

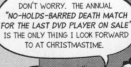

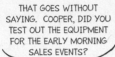

CRUSHED CHRISTMAS SPIRITS

The hardest thing you will have to deal with as you progress through the long, long, *long* holiday season is the increasingly bitter and irritated disposition of the customers. The closer it gets to Christmas, the grumpier people become and the worse they behave. Instead of "the most wonderful time of the year," it should more appropriately be called "the most likely time of the year to get your ass kicked over a parking space."

The most infuriating thing about all the holiday stress your patrons are kind enough to share with you is that it's completely self-imposed. People create their own problems, then take out their frustrations on you. Everyone acts like buying presents at Christmastime is this inescapable, mandatory thing that they have no choice but to suffer through. As if they were being forced to fight through crowds to buy useless trinkets under duress.

This all begs a simple question—if people are so tired of the grotesque over-commercialization of Christmas, then why don't they just stop participating in it?

The fact of the matter is that they can't. Most people are so trapped in their own materialistic nature that they simply can't picture a Christmas without presents. Instead, they go on creating this impossible standard for themselves and their families to make each holiday season bigger and better than the last, setting themselves up for inevitable disappointment. Subconsciously they know they're trapped in their own pointless and self-destructive behavior, so they act out their anger on others and treat you like you're just part of the machine that's causing their misery.

When you've sold out of the "it" gift of the season, the customers who missed out will act as though you personally ruined their Christmas. Like you should be responsible for the manufactured importance they've placed on a single product. *"Damn it, Nickelodeon told my daughter she wants a Baby Alive for Christmas, so you should damn well have it in stock!"*

When the expensive gifts they want are out of their financial reach, they'll act as though you're personally responsible for adding to their holiday debt. *"Why the hell do your fifty-five-inch plasma screens cost so much? You bastards won't be happy until you break me!"*

When they have to wait in long lines, they'll act as if you just don't know how to do your job. *"Why is this taking so long? Can't you service 200 people on four registers any faster?"*

In short, be prepared to get saturated with negative energy throughout the holiday season and have the Christmas spirit crushed right out of you.

Retail ruins Christmas.

'Twas the day before Christmas,
when all through the mall,
Disgruntled shoppers
filled up every hall.

They bustled and hurried
in manner unpleasant,
In an effort to buy
a few last-minute presents.

For each year when their children
looked under their trees,
They found them becoming
much harder to please.

Last year they had to buy
Sony Playstations
And iPods and laptops
to force their elation.

So this year they had to
search every last store
If they wanted to one-up
the Yuletide before.

And they shouted, "Bah humbug!
I'm not having fun!
I'm so sick of Christmas!
I'll be glad when it's done!"

Then a store clerk did grumble,
"I have it far worse!
For me it's been Christmas
since October first!

"You can leave if you want to,
but I have to stay!
Your materialism
has made things this way!

"Go home and spend time
with your loved ones, I say!
It's the most valuable gift
you can give anyway!

"Don't worry if the presents
you purchased are spurned ...

"... I'll be back in a day
to take all your returns."

MERRY
CHRISTMAS

CHAPTER 17

G.O.B.
(Going Out of Business)

C orporate mismanagement can doom a retailer to failure in spite of its employees' best efforts. For all the emphasis that is placed on your responsibility to make sales and follow rules, it is always the people in the home office who ultimately cause their own downfall through lack of common sense and true business acumen. In a corporate culture that routinely squanders billions of dollars, it's a wonder that any retailers manage to survive.

WHY THIS IS THE BEST THING
THAT COULD HAPPEN TO YOU

When you get the "bad" news that your store or company is going under, the reality that you will soon be out of a job can hit you like a ton of bricks. Contrary to your instincts however, this is the best thing that can happen to you during your retail career.

Why is losing your job in this way a good thing in retail? Let me count the ways.

1. It's a rock-solid alibi.

In all statistical probability, you will eventually get fed up with the special brand of nonsense your retailer habitually doles out and start looking for another job. During that search you will inevitably be asked why you've chosen to leave your current place of employment. This is always a tricky question to answer because your interviewer is liable to be turned off by the truth. Their home office/manager dishes out plenty of absurdity, too, so telling them you have a low tolerance for such things won't exactly endear you to them.

The beauty of your store going under is that you don't have to struggle to make up some bogus reason for leaving—you have no choice. Now you can safely pretend that you had a great attitude about your job and were the biggest team player in the world. Nobody has to know how much you openly hated it. You're leaving because you have to, not because you want to.

Think of it as forcing you to do what you will inevitably do yourself, except in a really convenient and neutral way that doesn't make you look like you have an attitude problem.

This is absolutely the easiest way out of any retail job.

2. Your job just got a whole lot easier.

When a store goes bankrupt, it can take several months to liquidate all the merchandise. During that time a liquidation company will take over and throw up big "Store Closing" and "All Sales Final" signs. They'll tell you not to take any more returns and instruct you what percentage to discount all the merchandise, but otherwise they'll leave you alone.

You'll be free to act and dress however you want. You can show up late, eat and drink behind the counter, leave the place a mess—nobody cares. Your attitude isn't going to scare anyone away when everything is 75 percent off.

If you're a manager, they might even give you a bonus if you don't quit before the final day. When Learningsmith went out of business, they paid me an extra $800 on top of my regular salary just to stay until the end. It was the only time they ever paid me a bonus. For two months I hung around, did absolute crap, answered to no one and was rewarded with a big chunk of cash on my way out—I felt like a CEO! It's awesome. I can't recommend it enough.

3. You don't have to take crap from anyone.

Without fear of consequences, you no longer have to pretend the customer is always right. In fact, you can tell them flat out how wrong they are. Your store is closing. There won't be anyone left to give you a bad reference. You have free rein to tell it like it is.

This is your short window of opportunity, so don't blow it. Once the liquidation is over you'll have to get a retail job somewhere else and put your kid gloves back on, so be sure to seize on this opportunity to give somebody the tongue-lashing they truly deserve.

All Sales Final

We got the news that Learningsmith was filing for bankruptcy in early December of 1999. It was no secret that the company was having financial trouble. Most of us had heard rumors for months, so when an "urgent" conference call for all stores in the district was suddenly announced one afternoon, we were hardly surprised by the bad news.

The managers on duty in every store in our district listened as some company bigwig whose title I don't recall explained the situation and told us how everything would go down. We regret to inform you . . . liquidation will begin immediately . . . thank you all for your hard work . . . don't talk to the media . . . blah, blah, blah. After that a couple of other bigwigs took turns consoling us, then our regional manager finished up the call by reading us a poem about how it's better to try and fail than to never try at all. That's right, a freakin' poem! Their gross incompetence had bankrupted the company and put us all out on the street for Christmas, and they were afraid *we* might feel bad about failing—like we were a bunch of third graders who just lost a little league game.

One of the managers spoke up just before the call ended. "*We* didn't fail anything," she huffed. "We did *our* jobs."

In typical fashion, this was greeted with some *tsk-tsk*ing from the DM and other assorted bigwigs. Corporate never hesitated to reprimand the store employees over every inane petty issue, but try to criticize *them* over something completely legitimate and it's suddenly considered poor form—a negative attitude. I forget to greet a customer at the door and I'm a dick. They drive the company into chapter 11 and we're supposed to just let it go. Yeah, that's fair.

Nobody pursued any name-calling after that. There was no real point in it anyway. Whether they copped to it or not, we all knew the score. They could hardly cover up their incompetence now. No thugs in a purple Learningsmith van would show up to abduct the voice of dissent on this fine day.

A few days later, the liquidation company was in control and their representative in our district showed up with a bunch of signs and told us how things were going to work. The registers were reprogrammed to print ALL SALES FINAL in bold letters on the bottom of the receipts, and signs to the same effect were hung everywhere. All merchandise started at 30 percent off and they told us we would get a phone call letting us know when to switch to 40 percent, then 50 percent, and so on.

The liquidation guy in charge of our store told us we could no longer accept returns or exchanges on any merchandise purchased from that point forward. He gave us a phone number to give to any customers who had a problem with it. "If anyone gives you crap, just have them call me at this number," he told us. "It goes to a dummy voice mail that I just delete every day. I don't even listen to it. Fuck 'em, they can read the signs."

I knew then and there that this was going to be sweet!

It was the height of the Christmas shopping season, so even at 30 percent off things were selling pretty fast. One super busy day about a week and a half into the liquidation, a lady came to my register and took a wooden chess set out of the Learning-smith bag she was carrying.

She placed it on the counter. "I need to return this."

"When did you buy it?" I asked.

"Yesterday," she replied.

I tapped the Plexiglas sign that was standing on the counter next to the register. "I'm sorry ma'am, but all sales are final."

"What?" she said, shocked, as if she couldn't see the giant red-and-yellow GOING OUT OF BUSINESS signs that were wall-papering the store. "No, that sign wasn't there yesterday."

"Yes, it was," I said flatly. I wasn't in the mood for this. There was a huge line and I had already been working all day. I was going to be out of a job in a few weeks, so I didn't need to take any lip from her.

"No, I want my money back for this," she said obstinately. "I have my receipt. You *have* to let me return it."

"No, I don't," I said, holding my ground. "The signs clearly say, 'all sales final.' You agreed to those terms, so you're out of luck."

"No, I need to return this," she insisted stubbornly.

"Look, there's nothing I can do," I said, turning out my hands and shrugging my shoulders. "The liquidation company is in charge now. If you want to talk to them, I can give you an eight-hundred number to call, but I can't do anything for you."

"No, those signs weren't here yesterday," she said shaking her head. "I had no way of knowing that all sales were final, so you have to let me return it."

I'd had enough. The signs had been up for almost two weeks. It was time to humiliate her. "Do you have your receipt?" I asked, with a sigh of mock defeat.

"Yes," she said, quickly fishing it out of the bag. Thinking she had won, she handed it to me with a smug grin.

I took the slip and immediately held it up to her so she could read the bold black letters at the bottom. "See? It says *all sales final* right on your receipt, so stop pretending that you didn't know anything about it." I put the receipt on top of her chess set and pushed it slightly toward her on the counter. "There's nothing I can do for you." The guy behind her in line covered his mouth to stifle a laugh.

Oh, she was pissed. "You have to let me return this! I *need* that money to buy Christmas presents!"

Now she was just getting ridiculous. The chess set cost $40 at regular price, meaning she only paid twenty-eight bucks for it at 30 percent off. If $28 is going to make or break your Christmas, then you should really be more judicious in the way you spend it.

"You shouldn't have bought it then," I said, annoyed.

The woman took a deep breath then exhaled heavily. "No," she said cocking her head to one side. She fluttered her eyes as if she were the one whose patience was being tried. "You *need* to let me return this."

If there's one thing I can't stand, it's someone who thinks the rules don't apply to them, so I lost it. "I'm done talking to you!" I shouted. "I don't know any other way to say it! You can't return this! You're stuck with it, so take it and go away!" I turned away from her and called to the next person in line, "Are you all set?" The next guy in line hesitated, not comfortable with jumping in the woman's grave just yet.

The woman grabbed her chess set and crammed it back in the bag. "No wonder you're closing! I hope you have a *horrible* Christmas!" she screamed, and stormed off.

Now that she was gone, the next guy in line finally approached the counter. "Wow, I hope you're not getting a lot of that."

"No more than usual," I said ringing up his stuff. "Now I just don't have to take it."

"No wonder you're closing" turned out to be the favorite catchphrase of any customer we had to lay the smack down on during the liquidation. As if we yelled at unreasonable customers all the time *before* we went bankrupt.

JUST DESERTS: A SHORT STORY

The shoe store with the backpack contest and 9:00 a.m. register-opening rule ran into financial trouble in the mid '90s. In an effort to save the company, they decided to close about half of their stores. Ours was one of them.

Since half of the stores were staying open, the strategy for the closing stores worked a little differently. All the closing stores shipped their current merchandise to the stores that were staying open, and then the company took all the ancient clearance merchandise they were drowning in and dumped it onto the closing stores for the liquidation.

I don't know if it ultimately saved the company, but the strategy certainly worked in the short run. Even though they sent us a mountain of horribly dusty, ugly hash from decades past, it was all ridiculously cheap, so it sold like hotcakes. Unfortunately, the quality of the merchandise attracted a crowd that was decidedly less pleasant than our previous clientele. We went from full-service men's shoe store to flea market in one day, so the adjustment period was simply awful.

My very first GOB sale was introducing me to whole new levels of rude that I never knew existed. The place was always packed with the dregs of society, constantly generating a mess that you could never stay on top of. It was not at all uncommon for a member of this new crowd to create a pile of ten to twenty pairs of loose shoes on the floor to sort through, then sit in the middle of the pile and literally toss the unwanted pairs over their shoulder.

One day I bought a box of donuts for the crew to enjoy and left it on the counter next to the register. Later that morning I was putting out more stock when I looked up just in time to catch some guy who was buying a big ugly pile of shoes brazenly reach over the counter, grab a donut and start eating it! I was absolutely incensed.

"*Hey!*" I yelled across the store at full volume.

The guy stopped dead in his tracks and looked at me guiltily. White powder fell from his lips as the whole store fell silent.

"*Did you just eat one of my donuts?*" I shouted in angry disbelief.

Before he could answer, I marched over to the counter, grabbed the box of donuts and plopped them on a box behind me and out of his reach. "What makes you think you can just take one of my donuts?" I demanded.

He pointed at the cashier with a shit-eating grin and shrugged. "I thought they were his."

"What the hell difference would that make?" I scolded. "Did *he* say you could have a donut?"

I looked at the cashier and his face told me he just wanted this to end. The poor guy had been ringing up a constant line of jerks all morning and now I was hovering over him and shouting at some dude over a freakin' donut. Aware that the stress was getting the better of me, I just walked away in a huff.

As I walked off the guy had the nerve to call after me, "Hey, can I get a discount for buying so many pairs?"

"You just ate your discount!" I shouted, and disappeared into the stockroom.

Weeks later, we had finally sold down to a few boxes of shoes. The DM called one day to see how we were doing. "What are you guys down to?" he asked.

"About three cases," I answered. I had never liked the guy. He had been a jerk to me since day one. He was always coarse and demanding and an all-around ball-busting prick. The only reason I was still treating him with any respect was because I needed a good reference to get another job.

"All right," he said. "Tell Mark I'll be there tomorrow to sign off on the place. You won't have anything left by then. That'll be your last day."

I decided this would be as good a time as any to ask for that reference. "Okay. Hey, I've been meaning to ask you if I could put you down as a reference, or if you could possibly write me a letter of recommenda . . ."

"Nope," he said, cutting me off. "Sorry, it's against company policy."

"What?" I said, stunned. "Are you serious?"

"Yeah, I'm serious," he replied. "Company policy. We can't

say anything about you, good or bad. The only thing we'll tell someone is when you were hired, and when you left."

"But the store will be closed," I tried to reason. "There won't be anybody for an employer to contact for a personal reference. That's going to be awkward to explain. Can't you make an exception in this case?"

"Nope," he said automatically. "My hands are tied. Look, don't worry about it. You'll be fine. I've got some more calls to make, so I'll see you tomorrow."

"But," I said, and he hung up.

Gene, a coworker and friend of mine, had just walked in as I was hanging up the phone. He hadn't worked in a couple of days, so he saw there was a drastic difference in the number of shoes we had left. "Wow," he said looking around. "I can't believe we sold all that crap."

"I know," I agreed. "I just got off the phone with the DM. He said tomorrow is going to be our last day."

"Really?" he asked curiously. "Is that case of toilet paper still in the back?"

I thought for a moment. "Yeah, I think so."

"Since they're not going to use it, you mind if I grab it tonight?" he asked.

Normally I would have said no, but I was so disillusioned and pissed about the reference thing that I just shrugged. "Yeah, whatever. I don't care."

"Cool, thanks."

That night we sold all but the last twelve pairs of godawful shoes you've ever seen. On the way out, Gene and I wheeled the case of toilet paper out to his car and pitched it into his trunk, then put the dolly in his back seat, too, just for the hell of it. Screw it. They were just going to leave it behind when the store closed anyway.

The next morning, the whole staff came in and pretty much just waited for the DM to show up. When he did, he wrote off the last twelve pairs of shoes and told me to throw them in the Dumpster.

I piled them into a box and was just about to carry them to

the back when he stopped me. "Whoa, aren't you forgetting something?"

"What? I asked confused. "You already wrote them off, right?"

He grabbed a utility knife off the counter and held it out to me. "You have to cut them," he said with a raised eyebrow, as if this was clearly something I should know about.

"Cut them?" I asked, even more confused.

"Yeah," he said plucking a shoe out of the box. "You have to cut them so nobody can dig them out of the Dumpster and get them for free." He took the knife, poked it through the leather upper of the shoe, and sliced a big gash in it to demonstrate.

I was truly perplexed by his completely logic-free train of thought. "We're throwing them away," I said, looking at him like he was a lunatic. "We're out of business. Who cares if someone takes them at this point? Geez, if some poor bastard is willing to root through our smelly Dumpster for these ugly things, I think he deserves to have them, don't you?"

The DM looked at me and shook his head as if I was just some hopeless simpleton who didn't understand business. "We don't give anything away for free. Cut 'em up," he said matter-of-factly, and held out the knife to me again.

"Whatever," I snorted and did as he said. I took the shoes into the stockroom, dumped them in a pile, sat down, and started slicing them up. When I was done, I put them back in the box and carried them out to the Dumpster. As I pitched the shoes into the Dumpster, it stirred up a nasty cloud of flies. I tried to imagine the type of person who would be desperate enough to climb into a filthy Dumpster to get a pair of display-faded, blue, faux-suede, chukka boots in size 7 EEE, but couldn't.

As I walked back down the service hallway to the stockroom, I distinctly remember thinking to myself, "*Where do DMs come from? Where do you find a guy who will stick to the letter of every rule no matter how ridiculous it is? What planet does he live on? That guy is in serious need of a reality check.*"

No sooner did I think it, than I reentered the stockroom to see Gene covering his mouth tightly with his hand and practically convulsing to stifle laughter.

"What?" I asked him, looking around.

Gene pointed to the bathroom door with his free hand. Tears were streaming down his cheeks.

Before I could ask again, someone pounded loudly on the bathroom door from the inside. "*Hey!*" the DM shouted desperately from within the bathroom. "God damn it, is anybody out there?! There's no toilet paper in here!"

Not only had I helped Gene steal the last of the toilet paper, but we had run out of paper towels earlier that day as well, so the DM was forced to fish some used napkins out of the trash to wipe his ass with.

Thank you, retail gods!

FREE STUFF!

When your store goes under, it's important to leave with your integrity intact. Stealing is wrong. Just because you may feel you've been treated unfairly, doesn't give you the right to walk away with a bonanza of free merchandise. No matter how easy it is, or how tempting it might be to justify that the liquidation company is going to make money regardless of what you take, you should refrain from the five-finger discount and do the right thing. Don't let the situation get the better of you. Just walk away.

On the other hand, I think everyone recognizes that taking office supplies, fixtures, and other non-merchandise totally does *not* count as stealing and is fair game. Thanks to my previous employment at a plethora of retailers that went belly-up, I will never have to purchase another extension cord or power strip as long as I live. Packing tape? If I went through a roll every six months, I still wouldn't run out until 2035. Need to borrow seven hammers? No problem. That still leaves me with two.

If you think that even taking office supplies is wrong, well, fine. Just leave it behind for the mall management or the new tenants to take. I'm sure they'll appreciate it. If you want to be the only person in the world who pays for staples and paper clips . . . that's your business.

Epilogue

Every retail worker has a horror story. A story about a customer who was so unbelievably and unnecessarily rude that it's forever etched in their brain. This is my story.

I Don't Need Your Help
I used to manage a small men's dress shoe store in a mall. It was a full-service store, so we'd measure the customers' feet, lace up their shoes for them, put them on their feet—the whole nine yards.

One slow afternoon, I was working alone when a short man with a beard and mustache entered the store with his son of around twelve. The son immediately found a chair and started playing his Gameboy while the man poked around looking at shoes.

"Hi, how are you today?" I asked from behind the counter.

"I'm just looking!" snarled the man, shooting me a completely uncalled-for look of disgust. "Can't I just look?"

His son kept playing his Gameboy, completely unfazed by his father's inappropriate outburst.

"All right," I said defensively. "Let me know if you need anything." Hoping he would just look and leave at this point, I went back to my paperwork.

A few minutes later he walked up to the counter and plopped down a display shoe from our clearance rack. "Give me this in a size nine."

I was disappointed to see that I would have to wait on this hothead after all, and doubly so to see that the shoe he wanted in a size nine was a long-ago-discontinued model that we would not likely have left in anything close to a common size.

"Sure," I said, and took the shoe into the stockroom.

Of course when I got back there we only had two pairs of the clearance shoe left. A seven and an eleven and a half. These shoes had been marked down multiple times over the years and were now dirt-cheap, so there wasn't anything of comparable price I could show him. Against all odds, however, there was a size nine in the same style shoe in a different color. Since my only other choice would have been to bring him a shoe that was five times as expensive, and this guy already had an attitude, I decided to take my chances with the alternate color.

Bracing myself for more flak, I reemerged with the shoes and walked over to where the man was now sitting. "I'm sorry, I didn't have a nine in that color, but I did have it in brown in that size. Would you like to try that?"

"Yeah, okay," he said calmly and casually.

"All right," I said, surprised by how well he was taking it. I knelt down, took one shoe out of the box, and began to lace it up, when he suddenly became annoyed and reached for the shoe.

"I can do it!" he barked angrily, as he literally ripped the shoe out of my hands.

"O-kay," I said, piqued, and stood up to wait for him to do it himself.

I hadn't been on my feet for more than ten seconds when he stopped his angry fumbling with the lacing to glare up at me from the chair. "Do you have to hover over me like that?" he shouted. "I don't need your help!"

I couldn't believe how needlessly belligerent this guy was. Disgusted and angry, I just walked back to the counter. *To hell with this guy,"* I thought. *"You don't want my help? Fine, you prick. I'm good with that."* Determined to let the guy rot in his chair, I went back to my paperwork a second time.

No such luck. After trying on the shoe, he spoke up in his calm voice again. "Okay, I like it," he said coaxingly. "If you can get it for me in the other color, you have yourself a sale."

Yeah, right. The shoe was discontinued and couldn't be ordered. Having worked in just about every store we had in the state, I also knew for a fact that nobody else in our district stocked this ancient piece of crap.

"Well, I can't order it," I said flatly. "It's discontinued."

"What does that mean?" he said crassly. He looked at me as if I had intentionally used some big esoteric word that nobody had ever heard of.

"It's a discontinued style," I explained. "They don't make it anymore."

"Well, call another store then," he demanded.

There was no use explaining to him that I already knew nobody else had it. He wouldn't have believed it anyway. "All right." I sighed and picked up the phone.

I called the next closest store and asked them to check to see if they had the shoe, which of course they didn't. After only one call, it suddenly struck me how stupid it was to waste any more time on this jerk. I wasn't going to uselessly call a bunch of stores just to appease him.

"Look," I said, "this shoe has been discontinued for a while, so it could take me some time to find. The best I can do is put out a computer search for it and call you if I turn up anything."

At that his eyes widened and his face turned beet red. "I want your supervisor on the phone!" he bellowed. "You only made *one* attempt to find that shoe! Is this how you run a business?"

Unbelievable. This guy was a real piece of work. Indignantly, I flipped over one of my business cards, and scrawled my district manager's voice mail number onto it. "Fine," I said angrily. "You want to call my supervisor? Go right ahead. Here's his number." I slid the card across the counter to him.

"No," he said putting his chubby little finger right in my face. "I want *you* to call him . . . *right now*!"

My threshold for abuse had been officially breached.

"You know what?" I said earnestly. "You're an asshole."

"Excuse me?!" he said, shocked and wide-eyed.

"You're an asshole," I repeated. "You've been rude to me since the moment you stepped in here." I slid the card toward him again. "If you want to call my district manager you go right ahead, but I'm not calling anybody. Now get out," I said, and pointed at the door to accentuate it.

The man just stood there for a moment with his mouth open. Being stood up to was obviously not something to which he was accustomed. Mad and sputtering, he picked up the business card, ripped it in half, and threw it in my general direction. He then chucked me the bird, yelled, *"Fuck you, you faggot!"* and stormed out.

This was enough to finally draw junior's attention from his video game. He sat there stupefied by the events for a moment as his dad left, then scampered after him like a frightened squirrel.

Although I still relive the anger whenever I tell that story, I consider standing up to that bastard the single most shining moment of my retail career.